Kennedy's Last Stand: Eisenhower, UFOs, MJ-12 & JFK's Assassination

Kennedy's Last Stand:
Eisenhower, UFOs, MJ-12 & JFK's Assassination

Michael E. Salla, M.A., Ph.D.

www.ExopoliticsInstitute.org
Kealakekua, Hawaii, USA

Kennedy's Last Stand:
Eisenhower, UFOs, MJ-12 & JFK's Assassination

Published by the Exopolitics Institute
PO Box 2199
Kealakekua, HI 96750 USA

ISBN-13: 978-0-9822902-6-2
ISBN-10: 0-9822902-6-8

Library of Congress Control Number 2013951676

Printed in the USA

Author's Website: www.Exopolitics.org

Publisher's Website: www.ExopoliticsInstitute.org

Cover Design: A.S. Whitecliff

Contents

Table of Figures xi

Dedication xv

Acknowledgements xvii

Introduction 1

   Endnotes – Introduction 10

Chapter 1 11

Did Kennedy Learn the Truth about UFOs and Alien Life from Secretary of the Navy, James Forrestal? 11

   Introduction 11

   Operation Paperclip 15

   James Forrestal, Operation Paperclip and John F. Kennedy ...21

   Was Forrestal Killed to Prevent Him Revealing the Truth about Extraterrestrial Life? 23

   Endnotes Chapter 1 31

Chapter 2 33

Eisenhower and Kennedy Receive Briefings on Roswell Flying Saucer Crash in 1947 33

   World Awakes to News of a Flying Saucer Crash at Roswell 33

   Flying Saucer Crash at Roswell 34

   General Eisenhower and Roswell Flying Saucer Crash 40

   Interplanetary Phenomenon Unit Report and the Kennedy Briefing 43

   The Haut Affidavit and the Interplanetary Phenomenon Unit Report 51

   Eisenhower and Kennedy were Briefed about the 1947 Roswell Crash 53

Endnotes Chapter 2 57

Chapter 3 59

President Eisenhower, MJ-12, S-4 and the Military Industrial
Complex 59

    Official Government Documents Supporting the Existence of
    the Majestic-12 Group... 65

    Eisenhower's Response to his Classified UFO Briefing......... 68

    The CIA and Area 51 72

    Whistleblower Testimonies about S-4 75

    CIA and S-4 Facility at Area 51 82

    Eisenhower's Confrontation with MJ-12 over S-4 84

    Endnotes Chapter 3 88

Chapter 4 93

Eisenhower Warns Kennedy about MJ-12 93

    John F. Kennedy Elected U.S. President............................... 93

    Eisenhower's Public Warning about the Military-Industrial
    Complex 96

    Eisenhower Privately Warns Kennedy about MJ-12 101

    Endnotes Chapter 4 106

Chapter 5 107

President Kennedy Challenges MJ-12 over Access to UFO Files
and Projects 107

    Taking Control of Cold War Psychological Operations 107

    Kennedy Approaches the CIA Director Dulles for Information
    on Majestic 12.. 110

    Dulles and the Burned MJ-12 Memorandum 115

    Conclusion: The CIA/MJ-12 Refusal to Cooperate with
    Kennedy... 122

Endnotes Chapter 5 124

Chapter 6 127

Who Were Majestic-12 Members During the Kennedy
Administration? 127

MJ-1: Allen Dulles 130

MJ-2: Dr. Edward Teller 131

MJ-3: Lt. General Marshall Carter 132

MJ-4: General Curtis LeMay 133

MJ-5: Lt. General Gordon Blake 134

MJ-6: Dr. Detlev Bronk 135

MJ-7: Dr. Jerome Hunsaker 136

MJ-8: Vice Admiral Laurence Frost 137

MJ-9: Gordon Gray 137

MJ-10: Dr. Donald Menzel 138

MJ-11: Lt. General John Samford 138

MJ-12: Dr. Lloyd Berkner 140

Majestic 12 in Different Presidential Administrations 140

Endnotes Chapter 6 143

Chapter 7 145

Kennedy Does an End Run around the CIA to Learn about UFOs
.... 145

Introduction 145

Robert Kennedy Secretly Briefed about Extraterrestrial Life
.... 146

Whistleblower Reports that President Kennedy Saw UFO
Crash Wreckage and Alien Artifacts 149

Did Kennedy Receive Messages from and Meet with
Extraterrestrials? 152

Conclusion: Kennedy's CIA End-Run Partly Succeeds 155

Endnotes Chapter 7 157

Chapter 8 159

Marilyn Monroe Death Connected to Kennedy Brothers and UFOs 159

Introduction.................................. 159

The Kennedy Brothers and Marilyn Monroe..................... 160

Monroe Plans Tell All Press Conference with Red Diary.... 166

Robert Kennedy Searches for Monroe's Red Diary 169

Eventual Confirmations of Kennedy Visits..................... 170

Monroe Knew about the Kennedys' UFO Secrets.............. 175

Is the CIA Wiretap Document Authentic? 179

Conclusion: Monroe Becomes a Victim of the UFO Cover Up 183

Endnotes - Chapter 8 186

Chapter 9 189

Kennedy's Attempt to Cooperate with the USSR on Space and UFOs 189

Introduction.................................. 189

Kennedy Proposes Joint Space and Lunar Missions with the Soviet Union 196

Kennedy's Hotline Conversation with Nikita Khrushchev .. 204

President Kennedy's UFO Initiatives Lead to Implementation of Assassination Directive 207

CIA Counterintelligence and the Kennedy Assassination ... 210

Endnotes Chapter 9 217

Chapter 10 221

Kennedy's Last Stand 221

Endnote Chapter 10 230
Index 231
About the Author..237
Other Books by Michael E. Salla, Ph.D...................................238

Table of Figures

Figure 1. Secretary Forrestal (center front row) at the New Reich Chancery in summer 1945. Kennedy in background. Source: JFK Presidential Library. 13

Figure 2. Alleged memo from General Marshal to President Roosevelt...............19

Figure 3. Hoover's Handwritten comment on FBI Memo 20

Figure 4. President Kennedy at the grave of James Forrestal, May 30, 1963. Source: JFK Presidential Library...............29

Figure 5. First News Report on July 8, 1947 33

Figure 6. Major Jesse Marcel crouches over weather balloon remains...............38

Figure 7. General of the Army Dwight D. Eisenhower in 1947. Source: Eisenhower Presidential Library...............41

Figure 8. Official U.S Navy Portrait of Lt John F. Kennedy. Source: JFK Presidential Library 44

Figure 9. Cover Page showing IPU Report. Allegedly Reclassified in 1960. Source: Majestic Documents 46

Figure 10. Truman Memo. Source: Majestic Documents...........61

Figure 11. Eisenhower Briefing Document, p. 2. Majestic Documents...............63

Figure 12. Initial Members of Majestic-12 Group 64

Figure 13. Cutler Twining Memo. Source: Majestic Documents 67

Figure 14. Area 51 with S-4 facility 74

Figure 15. Screen Shot from Alien Interview Video...............79

Figure 16. President Eisenhower meets President-Elect Kennedy on Dec 6, 1960...............93

Figure 17. Screenshot of Eisenhower's Farewell Address 97

Figure 18. President Eisenhower and President-Elect Kennedy at their January 19, 1961 Meeting...............104

Figure 19. Kennedy's Memo to CIA Director Dulles. Source: Majestic Documents 111

Figure 20. DCI Dulles responds to Kennedy's June Memorandum. Source: Majestic Documents...............114

Figure 21. Top Secret CIA Memo allegedly rescued from a fire. Source: Majestic Documents 118

Figure 22. Draft Project Environment Directive. Source: Majestic Documents 120

Figure 23. Cover Letter to Burned Directives Memorandum. Source: Majestic Documents 127

Figure 24. Table of Likely MJ-12 Members during different Presidential administrations and drafting of Assassination Directive 141

Figure 25. MJ-12 Group During first year of Kennedy Adminsitration 142

Figure 26. President Kennedy arrives at Homestead Air Force Base – 11/25/1962 150

Figure 27. John and Robert Kennedy having a tense conversation with Marilyn Monroe on May 9, 1962. Source: JFK Presidential Library 160

Figure 28. Hoover meets with President Kennedy and Attorney General Kennedy in Feb 1961. Source: JFK Library 164

Figure 29. Alleged CIA document summarizing wiretaps of Marilyn Monroe. Source: Majestic Documents 176

Figure 30. Transcript of CIA Wiretap Summary 177

Figure 31. Burleson's computer enhanced version reveals name of Gen Shulgen. Source: Majestic Documents 181

Figure 32. Kennedy meets Eisenhower at Camp David, April 22, 1961. Source: JFK Presidential Library 193

Figure 33. Kennedy and Khrushchev met in Vienna on June 4, 1961. Source: JFK Presidential Library 195

Figure 34. President Kennedy addressing United Nations General Assembly. Sept 25, 1961. Source: JFK Presidential Library ... 197

Figure 35. NSAM 271. Source: Majestic Documents 200

Figure 36. Kennedy Draft Memorandum to CIA Director, McCone. Source: Majestic Documents 202

Figure 37. NSA Hotline Intercept. P.1. Source: Majestic Documents 206

Figure 38. Handwriting at bottom of Kennedy Memorandum to CIA Director, McCone, Nov 12, 1963. "Response from Colby –

Angleton has the directive." 11/20/63. Source: Majestic
Documents...210

Dedication

To James V. Forrestal and John F. Kennedy, friends and allies who sought to inform the world of the truth that we are not alone, and paid the ultimate price.

Acknowledgements

I owe a great debt to the work of Dr. Robert Wood and Ryan Wood in researching, authenticating and making available the Majestic Documents. In particular, I thank their efforts in analyzing the Burned Memo which is so critical for uncovering the role of the Majestic-12 Group in the assassination of John F. Kennedy. I am also grateful to Dr. Wood for his corrections of an earlier version of this book. I also wish to thank Stanton Friedman, M.Sc., for his own valuable efforts in researching and authenticating the Eisenhower Briefing Document, the Truman Memo and the Cutler-Twining Memo. In particular, his work in determining the validity of the thirteen individuals named in the historic evolution of Majestic-12 at the time of the President Eisenhower's multiple briefings in November 1952 was very helpful.

I also wish to thank Dr. Donald Burleson for his valuable contribution in authenticating the validity of the CIA Wiretap Memo. His computer enhanced image analysis yielded important new data for helping validate this document.

I also wish to thank Thomas Carey and Donald Schmitt for authenticating the Roswell UFO crash, and making available the affidavit of Walter Haut. His eyewitness testimony was very helpful in validating one of the key Majestic documents used in this book.

I am indebted to the many brave whistleblowers who have come forward to give their eyewitness accounts of what they saw and experienced in various projects concerning extraterrestrial life and technology. In particular I thank Robert Lazar, Derek Hennessy, Col. Steve Wilson, Dan Burisch, and Michael Kruvant Wolf for their testimonies concerning the S-4 facility at Area-51. I also wish to thank "Kewper" and Stephen Lovekin for sharing their eyewitness accounts of President Eisenhower's dissatisfaction with the way classified UFO projects were being run during his administration.

I am grateful to the John F. Kennedy Presidential Library for making available their facilities and resources during my visit, and for making available to the public domain, photographs of President Kennedy.

I am especially grateful to Kathleen Osmon, Stuart Ward and Yvette Baeu for their diligence and support in proofreading. Kathleen's speed and thoroughness helped me easily meet my publishing deadline. Stuart and Yvette were very helpful with their editorial suggestions that helped remove many redundancies. Their collective corrections and suggestions have been invaluable for improving the quality of this book.

I am also indebted to John Adelmann for his additional proof reading and editorial suggestions that provided further improvements for the benefit of readers.

Finally, I wish to thank the wonderful soulmate life has blessed me with, Angelika S. Whitecliff, for designing the cover; and helping edit and proofread earlier versions of this book. Her encouragement in fully identifying the role of James Forrestal, in a formative period in the life of John Kennedy, was particularly helpful.

Introduction

Just before beginning his first term on January 20, 1993, President-Elect Clinton made a very strange request to close family friend and lawyer Webster Hubbell: "If I put you over there in ustice I want you to find the answer to two questions for me: One, who killed JFK. And two, are there UFOs."[1] According to Hubbell, "Clinton was dead serious."[2] Finding answers to these two questions appeared to be very important for Clinton and his future presidency. Why else would he assign a trusted friend to a senior position in the Department of Justice to find answers to questions most often asked by fringe conspiracy theorists?

We do know that Clinton did go on to assign Webster Hubbell to the Department of Justice on the first day of the new Presidential administration. We know that Clinton wanted to appoint Hubble to the top job as Attorney General, but finally had to settle for Associate Attorney General. Nevertheless, as the third highest ranking official in the Department of Justice, Hubble enjoyed impressive executive powers and security clearances to find answers to Clinton's questions. Hubbell would eventually write about Clinton's strange request and what he was able to find out in his memoirs, *Friends in High Places*.[3]

We don't know why Clinton asked Hubble to find the answers to these two questions. Was it just curiosity over two unrelated issues: the death of a childhood hero, and Clinton's private interest in UFOs? Or did Clinton believe there was some link between Kennedy's death and the UFO issue? Was Clinton using Hubble to test the bureaucratic waters to find if there was indeed such a link, in order to fathom how far he, himself, could go in learning about the UFO issue?

1

There have long been rumors of a link between the Kennedy assassination and the UFO issue. Veteran UFO researcher and Emmy Award winner, Linda Moulton Howe, for example, was confidentially told of such a link by intelligence sources:

> I had been told by two different government intelligence agents in two different parts of the United States that John F. Kennedy had been assassinated on November 22, 1963 on orders of the CIA because after a long and tense period of grievances that included the controversial pull back of American air cover at the Bay of Pigs, JFK - based on some firsthand knowledge from his service as a U. S. Naval intelligence officer - had demanded access to all files and images concerning an extraterrestrial presence on earth.[4]

How plausible is the idea that Kennedy was assassinated because of his efforts to learn about UFOs and extraterrestrial life? Also, did Kennedy learn about extraterrestrial life during the World War II era as a result of his service with U.S. Naval Intelligence?

What we do know for certain is that Webster Hubbell said that he was stymied in his efforts to find satisfactory answers to Clinton's two questions. Hubbell wrote: "I had looked at both [questions], but wasn't happy at the answers I was getting."[5]

Ultimately, Hubble had to resign on March 14, 1994, over a financial scandal involving his overbilling clients while serving as an attorney in Arkansas.[6] Was it just coincidence? Or was the one person in the Clinton administration actively seeking answers to who was behind the Kennedy assassination and the UFO issue removed from public office in a manufactured scandal by some mysterious behind-the-scenes force? We do know that

Hillary Clinton certainly believed that that there was a powerful group of individuals operating behind the scenes in a "vast right-wing conspiracy" that used manufactured scandals to achieve their political objectives.[7] The removal of Hubbell may well have been the first case of a manufactured scandal to undermine Clinton's efforts to learn about the Kennedy and UFO issues.

We do know from FOIA documents that Bill and Hillary Clinton were actively seeking answers to questions over the UFO issue.[8] FOIA documents reveal that both traveled in August 1995 to the Teton, Wyoming Ranch of Laurence Rockefeller and received an informal briefing about UFOs and extraterrestrial life. An August 4, 1995, memo by President Clinton's Science Advisor, Dr Jack Gibbons, confirmed that the Clintons would be vacationing with Rockefeller at his Teton Ranch in Wyoming that summer, and they would discuss UFOs:

> You will probably see Mr Rockefeller on your vacation in the Tetons. He will want to talk with you about his interest in extrasensory perception, paranormal phenomenon, and UFOs.[9]

In the memo, Gibbons then attempted to dissuade the Clintons from pursuing Rockefeller's agenda to disclose national security files concerning UFOs:

> He knows that we are trying to be helpful in responding to his concerns about UFO's and human potential … but I've made no secret about my conviction that we must not be too diverted from more earthly imperatives.[10]

The Clintons gave up their active quest to learn about UFOs as they decided it would adversely impact Bill's 1996 Presidential election prospects. In 2005, at a speech in Hong Kong, Bill

Clinton gave some details about his unsuccessful efforts to learn about UFOs a decade earlier:

> I did attempt to find out if there were any secret government documents that revealed things and if there were, they were concealed from me too. I wouldn't be the first president that underlings have lied to or that career bureaucrats have waited out. But there may be some career person somewhere hiding these dark secrets, even from elected Presidents. But if so, they successfully eluded me, and I am almost embarrassed to tell you that I did try to find out.[11]

In 2012, when contacted by various UFO researchers, Hubbell was evasive in answering questions about Clinton's strange request at the beginning of his administration. Presidential UFO researcher Grant Cameron described what happened:

> Hubbell was later questioned again by film producer James Fox, and all he would say is "You will have to talk to Bill Clinton." Recently reporter Billy Cox attempted to get Hubbell to explain what had happened by asking him a question about a long time CIA official, Chase Brandon, who came forward in 2012 to say that he had seen a box at CIA headquarters that confirmed the 1947 Roswell crash as an extraterrestrial event. At first Hubbell looked like he was ready to talk. "Thanks for your inquiry," Hubbell replied. "All of your questions will be answered." Later, however, when directly being asked about Clinton's request to find out about UFOs, the cheese on Hubbell's cracker appeared to slide off, "I think I made myself clear. No interviews, and that the answers to all your questions will be revealed. Have a good day."[12]

Hubbell's initial willingness to answer questions and subsequent evasiveness is perplexing. Was he warned off from answering any questions regarding his inquiries into the Kennedy Assassination and UFOs?

We do know that in his efforts to find answers to the question of who killed JFK, Hubbell had amassed a lot of documentation. In October, 2012, documentation accumulated by the Clinton administration on the Kennedy assassination was released by the Clinton Presidential Library in Little Rock, Arkansas. Canadian UFO researcher Grant Cameron wrote:

> After six and one half years of waiting, the Clinton Library in Little Rock, Arkansas has just released 7,663 pages of files on the assassination of former President John Kennedy in 1963. The files are being released in reply to an FOIA filed in February 2006. The Clinton Library is in charge of releasing the files of the Clinton administration to the public. [13]

In finding answers to the questions, who killed JFK and what is the truth behind the UFO issue, we need to go to the beginning of the modern UFO era. Specifically, reports that crashed UFOs were found during the World War II era, and that Nazi Germany had secretly worked on developing alien technologies as part of their war effort. Surprisingly, we find evidence that John F. Kennedy may have been exposed to sensitive information concerning these retrieved technologies and Nazi reverse engineering efforts. It is even possible that Kennedy may have physically seen some of these technologies during an official government fact-finding trip to Europe in the summer of 1945.

We then move to evidence concerning the Roswell flying saucer crash that was officially announced by the U.S. Army in an authorized Press release on July 8, 1947. In researching the Roswell UFO crash, we find evidence that two future Presidents,

Eisenhower and Kennedy, had received briefings about them. If the Roswell crash did involve an interplanetary space vehicle, then it is no surprise that General Eisenhower, then Army Chief of Staff, received a briefing. More surprising is the possibility that Kennedy, then a freshman Congressman, also received a briefing. Was it possible that Kennedy, because of his wartime experiences in Naval Intelligence, had learned about an extraterrestrial presence as Moulton Howe's intelligence sources contend? Perhaps he was exposed to some of these technologies during his 1945 trip to Germany. If so, it might explain why the freshman congressman was briefed about the Roswell crash.

In this book, I begin by examining Kennedy's World War II experiences in U.S. Naval Intelligence and his close relationship with the Secretary of the Navy, James Forrestal. Forrestal went on to become the first Secretary of Defense in 1947, until his removal and death in 1949. It will be revealed that Forrestal was given briefings about extraterrestrial life and technologies that he may have passed on to Kennedy. His mysterious death raises many questions about whether he was silenced for his revelations. Undoubtedly, Forrestal's death had a powerful impact on Kennedy who was then serving his second term in the U.S. Congress.

In the second chapter, I examine the Roswell UFO crash and the possibility that Eisenhower and Kennedy were both briefed about it. There is overwhelming testimonial and documentary evidence that the Roswell crash did involve extraterrestrial life and technology. The evidence supports the conclusion that Eisenhower and possibly Kennedy were briefed about it.

Chapter three examines the Eisenhower Presidency and what may have evolved over the thirteen years since the Roswell UFO crash and Kennedy winning the 1960 Presidential election. Of particular significance will be Eisenhower's alleged confrontation with a control group called Majestic-12, authorized by President Truman, to have responsibility over the issues of extraterrestrial life and technology. I examine Eisenhower's approval for the construction of Area 51 and its most highly classified facility, S-4; how MJ-12 made S-4 at Area 51 its main base of operations, and why the CIA was given responsibility for security at Area 51. Most importantly, I examine evidence that Eisenhower's farewell speech was a veiled reference to the power MJ-12 was accumulating from running the UFO/extraterrestrial issue.

The two private meetings between President Eisenhower and President-elect Kennedy, and what they likely shared about the UFO/extraterrestrial issue, is discussed in chapter four. In particular, I show why there is good reason to conclude that Eisenhower shared important specifics about his farewell speech warning about the danger posed by the Military-Industrial Complex.

Kennedy made various attempts to gain access to files concerning extraterrestrial life and technology. Chapter five discusses a series of executive actions Kennedy took early in his administration to this end. On February 19, 1961, Kennedy issued an Executive Order placing cold war psychological warfare programs under the control of his National Security Advisor. This order was followed on June 28 by a series of Presidential Memoranda to implement Presidential executive oversight over covert CIA operations through the Joint Chiefs of Staff. These executive actions coincided with Kennedy's efforts to gain access to the activities of a highly classified project dealing with UFOs and extraterrestrial life: MJ-12 Special Studies Project. Kennedy's executive actions led to a bitter conflict with his outgoing CIA Director, Allen Dulles who opposed granting Kennedy access. In order to prevent any repetition of events that threatened the operations of MJ-12 during the Eisenhower administration, Dulles drafted a set of directives in the summer of 1961. One of which was an assassination directive that could be used again senior U.S. political officials.

Chapter six reveals for the first time the most likely identities of those who authorized the MJ-12 assassination directive in late 1961. The identification of these public officials is highly significant. There is good reason to conclude that the directive was implemented two years later when President Kennedy was on the verge of succeeding in gaining access to the CIA's classified UFO files.

In chapter seven, I discuss actions Kennedy took to learn about UFOs and extraterrestrials despite lack of cooperation from CIA officials with access to classified UFO files and projects. Kennedy traveled to USAF bases to view extraterrestrial artifacts under the control of the Pentagon. He met civilians with knowledge about UFOs, and allegedly participated in a direct meeting with extraterrestrials. He worked closely with his brother, Bobby, who received secret briefings from a retired Army intelligence officer about UFOs. In this phase of his efforts to learn about UFOs, Kennedy worked with the U.S. military to learn as much as possible about UFO/extraterrestrial operations while being denied access to information and projects controlled by the CIA.

Marilyn Monroe's plans for a tell-all press conference regarding what she had been told about UFOs by President Kennedy is discussed in chapter eight. I show that Robert Kennedy was directly involved in events on the day of Monroe's death, and discuss evidence suggesting that her death was a botched attempt to silence her. Monroe's plans to publicly reveal some of the Kennedy brothers' UFO secrets was a direct threat to President Kennedy's efforts to assert control over information and projects involving extraterrestrial life.

The final phase of Kennedy's effort to assert authority over the UFO/extraterrestrial issue, which began on September 20, 1963, when Kennedy embarked on a high-risk political strategy of getting NASA to cooperate with the USSR on joint space and lunar missions, is revealed in chapter nine. Less well known is that this phase brought to a climax a confrontation with the CIA and those in control of the MJ-12 Special Studies Project, over the release of classified UFO files .

The final chapter describes Kennedy's last stand. Kennedy had a strong interest in UFOs and extraterrestrial life dating back to at least the Roswell Crash, and likely even further back to his experiences in a 1945 tour of post-war Germany. The information President Eisenhower had privately shared with him galvanized Kennedy into action to learn more. These actions culminated in a deadly behind-the-scenes confrontation with the CIA and the Majestic-12 Group in the final month of his life. Kennedy's last stand was a brave effort to wrest back firmly into Presidential control the ultimate authority over classified projects involving extraterrestrial life and technology.

Endnotes – Introduction

---

[1] Webster Hubbell, *Friends in High Places: Our Journey from Little Rock to Washington, D.C.* (William Morrow and Co., 1997).

[2] Webster Hubbell, *Friends in High Places: Our Journey from Little Rock to Washington, D.C.* (William Morrow and Co., 1997).

[3] Webster Hubbell, *Friends in High Places: Our Journey from Little Rock to Washington, D.C.*

[4] Linda Moulton Howe, "JFK, MJ-12 and Outer Space," http://presidentialufo.com/john-f-kennedy/73-president-kennedy-ufo-articles

[5] Webster Hubbell, *Friends in High Places: Our Journey from Little Rock to Washington, D.C.* (William Morrow and Co., 1997).

[6] See Wikipedia entry for Webster Hubbell, http://en.wikipedia.org/wiki/Webster_Hubbell

[7] Hillary Clinton first used the term "vast right-wing conspiracy" in her defense of Bill Clinton during the Lewinksy scandal and other campaigns against the Clinton administration. http://en.wikipedia.org/wiki/Vast_right-wing_conspiracy

[8] See Grant Cameron, "Extraterrestrial Politics Part 1 – Rockefeller Initiative to The Clinton White House," http://www.presidentialufo.com/bill-clinton/105-extraterrestrial-politics-part-1-rockefeller-initiative-to-the-clinton-white-house

[9] Source: http://www.hillaryclintonufo.net/documents/GibbonsClinton.jpg

[10] Source: http://www.hillaryclintonufo.net/documents/GibbonsClinton.jpg

[11] September 2005 to CLSA group in Hong Kong, http://www.presidentialufo.com/ufo-quotes

[12] Grant Cameron, http://www.presidentialufo.com/john-f-kennedy/468-kennedy-assassination-files-now-public . For a detailed article by Billy Cox on his email correspondence with Webster Hubbell, go to: http://devoid.blogs.heraldtribune.com/13291/riding-the-hubbell-ufo-roller-coaster/?tc=ar

[13] "Kennedy Assassination Files Now Public," http://www.presidentialufo.com/john-f-kennedy/468-kennedy-assassination-files-now-public

Chapter 1

Did Kennedy Learn the Truth about UFOs and Alien Life from Secretary of the Navy, James Forrestal?

Introduction

During World War II, John F. Kennedy's father arranged for his second son to be given a plum position in the Office of Naval Intelligence. In August, 1941, Joseph Kennedy wrote to Captain Alan Kirk, former naval attaché at the U.S. Embassy in London when Joseph Kennedy served as Ambassador to the United Kingdom (1938-40):

> I am having Jack see a medical friend of yours in Boston tomorrow for physical examination and then I hope he'll become associated with you in Naval Intelligence.[14]

Kirk, now head of the Office of Naval Intelligence in Washington, D.C., made the necessary arrangements. John F. Kennedy had earlier distinguished himself with a bestselling 1940 book, *Why England Slept*, based on his senior thesis at Harvard University.[15] Naval Intelligence was pleased to accept this "exceptionally brilliant student, [who] has unusual qualities and a definite future in whatever he undertakes."[16]

John F. Kennedy began his military service in October 1941 as an Ensign, responsible for collating reports from overseas stations for distribution in Office of Naval Intelligence bulletins. After being promoted to Lieutenant, he was transferred to the Pacific in command of a PT boat that was rammed and cut in two by a Japanese destroyer. Badly injured, Kennedy was able to lead six of his crew to safety. Only two crew members died. Newswire stories about the incident instantly made Kennedy a national war hero:

KENNEDY'S SON IS HERO IN PACIFIC AS DESTROYER SPLITS HIS PT BOAT, the *New York Times* disclosed. KENNEDY'S SON SAVES 10 IN PACIFIC; KENNEDY'S SON IS HERO IN THE PACIFIC, the Boston Globe announced with local pride.[17]

When the war was over, he was welcomed home as a hero.

With his national war hero status, family connections, and precocious intellect, Kennedy became friends with influential political and military leaders. He became particularly close to one of his father's friends, James Forrestal, who was Secretary of the Navy (1944-1947). Forrestal wanted to recruit Kennedy to his personal staff and included him as his guest in a tour of devastated Europe in the summer of 1945. According to historian Robert Dallek:

> The secretary, who knew Joe well and was greatly impressed by his twenty-eight-year-old son, wanted Jack to join his staff in the Navy Department. But first he invited Jack to go with him to Potsdam and then around Germany for a look at the destruction of its cities and factories from five years of bombing, and assess the challenges posed by rehabilitating a country divided into Russian and Western sectors. In the course of their travels, Jack met or at least saw up close many of the most important leaders of the day... When Forrestal's plane landed in Frankfurt, a journalist recalled, the plane doors opened, and out came Forrestal. Then, to my amazement, Jack Kennedy. Ike was meeting Forrestal. So Jack met Ike."[18]

Figure 1. Secretary Forrestal (center front row) at the New Reich Chancery in summer 1945. Kennedy in background. Source: JFK Presidential Library.

In the diary Kennedy kept of the trip, which he published as *Prelude to Leadership*,[19] Kennedy describes the August 1 meeting with Eisenhower:

> We flew from Bremen to Frankfurt and were met at the airport by a Battalion of Paratroopers and General Eisenhower... Eisenhower talked with Forrestal for a few minutes, and it was obvious why he is an outstanding figure. He has an easy personality, immense self-assurance, and gave an excellent presentation of the situation in Germany.[20]

The book's editor reveals how Kennedy became an observer of the Potsdam Conference attended by President Truman, Prime Minister Churchill and Premier Stalin in late July. Tensions were high as Truman had been warned to take a tough stand against the Soviets:

> It was into this charged atmosphere that Secretary of the Navy Forrestal, an uninvited guest, flew into Gatow Airport on July 28 with his friend, John F. Kennedy... Forrestal was deeply concerned about the Russian postwar machinations, both military and political ... It is a remarkable footnote to history that JFK probably had more "inside" information on crucial world events in July of 1945 than did the new president who was preparing for the Potsdam Conference.[21]

The "inside" information Kennedy was receiving during his 1945 trip with Forrestal was coming from the highest level: "Kennedy had the unique opportunity of meeting many of the key leaders on the international stage – Churchill, Eisenhower, Truman, Atlee, Beven, de Valera, and Gromyko."[22]

In a subsequent meeting with Eisenhower on July 29, Forrestal revealed in his own personal diaries, published posthumously, some of the discussions that occurred:

> On the Monday Forrestal breakfasted with the President – together with Eisenhower, Clay, Judge Samuel Rosenman, his own naval aides and others [possibly including Kennedy] - and what he recorded of the talk was interestingly enough in view of the meeting with the American armor, mainly about postwar military plans and policies.[23]

In these high level meetings with Eisenhower and the President, Secretary Forrestal was briefed about the most sensitive plans for post-war Germany. Among these plans was the recruitment of German scientists who worked on advanced technologies developed by Nazi Germany. They were going to be secretly repatriated under a covert program called "Operation Paperclip."[24] Forrestal was sharing this highly sensitive information with Kennedy. So what was Operation Paperclip?

Operation Paperclip

Operation Paperclip involved transferring scientific expertise and technologies pioneered by Nazi Germany to the United States. It was run by the Joint Intelligence Objectives Agency, comprised of intelligence officers from each of the military services.[25] Operation Paperclip was formally approved by President Truman in August 1945, soon after the Potsdam Conference. The timing is very significant. It meant that Eisenhower and his military commanders were able to persuade Truman that the U.S. needed the advanced scientific expertise and technologies developed in Nazi Germany.

Truman would have naturally asked why the victorious Allied powers would need the scientific expertise of the defeated Nazis? The answers he received from Eisenhower's military experts who had seen Nazi technologies were compelling. For example, Major-General Hugh Knerr, deputy commander of the U.S. Air Force in Europe, stated:

> Occupation of German scientific and industrial establishments has revealed the fact that we have been alarmingly backward in many fields of research. If we do not take the opportunity to seize the apparatus and the brains that developed it and put the combination back to

work promptly, we will remain several years behind while we attempt to cover a field already exploited.[26]

So what kind of technologies were these Nazi scientists involved in?

Chief among the scientific expertise sought by the U.S. was advanced rocketry. Nazi Germany's rocket program was highly effective with the V-1 and V-2 rockets that were used against Great Britain. Scientists, such as Werner Von Braun who developed these devastating weapons, were repatriated to start the U.S. rocket program. Decades later, Von Braun's Nazi past would be forgotten, and he would become a respected father of the Apollo program.

Another area of interest was the Nazi's development of flying saucer-shaped craft. There is much evidence that the Nazis had a highly advanced program based on a flying saucer design.[27] According to Virgil Armstrong, a former CIA agent:

> We know that in the early parts of the war there were certain factions of the Allied forces that did not believe he [Hitler] had a secret weapon and it wasn't until the Americans made much emphasis of this that they began to look at it seriously and indeed did discover that Hitler not only had a secret weapon, he had what we would call today a UFO or spacecraft.[28]

Armstrong's remarkable claim is supported by Captain Edward Ruppelt, responsible for the U.S. Air Force Project Bluebook, who claimed in 1956:

> When WWII ended, the Germans had several radical types of aircraft and guided missiles under development. The majority were in the most preliminary stages, but they were the only known craft that could even approach

the performance of objects reported to UFO observers...[29]

Were these highly advanced projects based solely on scientific breakthroughs by Nazi scientists, or had the Nazis discovered extraterrestrial technologies from around the world?

Professor Herman Oberth, who pioneered rocket design for Nazi Germany during World War II, moved to Peenemunde to work with Von Braun in developing the V-2 rocket. After the war, Oberth was asked why the Nazis had been so successful in their technology programs. He answered:

> "We cannot take the credit for our record advancement in certain scientific fields alone; we have been helped." When asked by whom, he replied: "The people of other worlds."[30]

As the Supreme Allied Commander for Europe during and immediately after World War II, Eisenhower was certainly briefed on reports about flying saucer technologies and Nazi efforts to develop them. Eisenhower very likely came across answers to whether or not such technologies were solely scientific developments by German scientists; or, as Oberth claimed, were based on extraterrestrial technologies.

Were some of these technologies related to extraterrestrial life? Were they related to the technologies retrieved by the U.S. during World War II? One allegedly leaked official document refers to the Department of Naval Intelligence's retrieval of an unidentified crashed craft of interplanetary origin after the February 24 and 25, 1942 Los Angeles Air Raid:

> ... regarding the air raid over Los Angeles it was learned by Army G2 that Rear Admiral Anderson... recovered an

17

unidentified airplane off the coast of California... with no bearing on conventional explanation... This Headquarters has come to the determination that the mystery airplanes are in fact not earthly and according to secret intelligence sources they are in all probability of interplanetary origin.[31]

The document is an alleged Top Secret Memorandum from Chief of Staff of the Army, George Marshall, to President Roosevelt dated March 5, 1942. If true, then the incident occurred while Kennedy was serving in the Department of Naval Intelligence. This raises the intriguing possibility that he had learned about the incident soon after it occurred. This possibility is supported by two intelligence sources, who Linda Moulton Howe claimed had told her that Kennedy's knowledge of extraterrestrial life was "based on some firsthand knowledge from his service as a U. S. Naval intelligence officer."[32]

Significantly, Forrestal was Undersecretary of the Navy at the time of the Los Angeles air raid incident, suggesting that he would have likely received an official briefing about the recovery. If not then, he would almost certainly have been briefed later when he was promoted to Navy Secretary on May 19, 1944. According to the document, Marshall:

> ... issued orders to Army G2 that a special intelligence unit be created to further investigate the phenomenon and report any significant connection between recent incidents and those collected by the director the office of Coordinator of Information. [33]

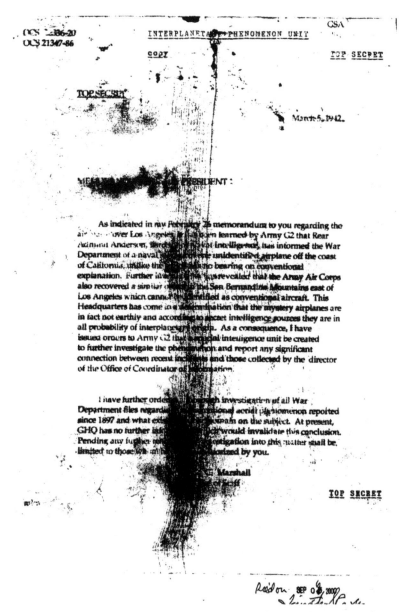

Figure 2. Alleged memo from General Marshal to President Roosevelt

Support for the authenticity of this document comes from none other than the Director of the FBI, J. Edgar Hoover. In an official memo released through the Freedom of Information Act, Hoover handwrote on July 15, 1947 (a week after the alleged Roswell UFO crash): "We must insist upon full access to disks recovered. For instance, in the La case the Army grabbed it and would not let us have it for cursory examination."[34] Was Hoover referring to a flying disc recovered after the Los Angeles Air Raid, or a disc recovered from the state of Louisiana (LA) prior to the Roswell incident? Whatever the answer, Hoover is indicating that the U.S. Army was studying recovered flying discs and not sharing information with the FBI.

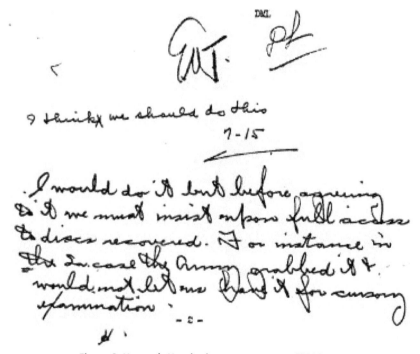

Figure 3. Hoover's Handwritten comment on FBI Memo

James Forrestal, Operation Paperclip and John F. Kennedy

As mentioned earlier, James Forrestal became Secretary of the U.S. Navy in 1944. He traveled to Germany to observe the Potsdam Conference and to see firsthand the situation in devastated Germany. As Navy Secretary, he would play a significant role in decisions being made about the Navy's participation in numerous planned projects, including Operation Paperclip. Paperclip was run by the Joint Intelligence Objectives Agency, which included U.S. Navy intelligence officers. They were Forrestal's subordinates and would brief him on various aspects of Operation Paperclip.

Forrestal, for example, visited the submarine facility in Bremen to determine the usefulness of Germany's submarine technology and production methods for the U.S Navy. Forrestal was accompanied by Kennedy who wrote about the Bremen visit:

> The harbor of Bremerhaven was full of captured ships…. Figures were given which showed German submarine production at about one a day….These submarines were all equipped with the Schuzzle breathing device which enable them to stay under water for long periods. One submarine on a 30 day cruise only surfaced four hours.[35]

Kennedy was Forrestal's guest, and was given access to high level officials to ask questions. On July 31, Kennedy wrote in *Prelude to Leadership*: "Spent the day in Bremen talking to Navy officials and to the heads of military government in this area." [36]

Kennedy was asked to give his advice on various German technologies that might be applicable for U.S. deployment. One of Kennedy's areas of expertise was the Navy's collection of PT boats. He had this to say about the German equivalent:

[T]he German E boat was far superior to our PT boat. It was 25 feet longer, just as fast, nearly twice as heavy, and had greater cruising range at high speed – in armaments it was about equal.[37]

In his tour of Germany and captured Nazi technologies, Forrestal very likely witnessed some of the alleged flying saucer and/or extraterrestrial technologies, firsthand. As Navy Secretary, he certainly had the rank and need to know about such technologies and their potential relevance to the U.S. Navy. If Forrestal did witness some of these advanced flying saucer/extraterrestrial technologies, he would certainly have shared the information with Kennedy. It is also highly likely that he would have allowed Kennedy to also witness some of these captured technologies, firsthand.

Such a conclusion is supported by the two intelligence sources mentioned earlier that told Linda Moulton Howe that Kennedy's knowledge of extraterrestrial life was "based on some firsthand knowledge from his service as a U. S. Naval intelligence officer."[38] If Howe's sources are correct, it is most likely that Kennedy gained this "firsthand knowledge" from the 1942 Los Angeles Air Raid incident, and then his 1945 summer tour of post-war Europe while traveling with Forrestal. Kennedy was likely briefed about Project Paperclip by Forrestal, and even learned firsthand that some of the Nazi technologies were based on flying saucers and/or were extraterrestrial in origin.

In September 1947, Forrestal would go on to become the First Secretary of the Department of Defense. Significantly, he also became one of the founding members of a secret control group authorized to take charge of extraterrestrial related projects. I will discuss this control group further in chapter three.

The existence of this control group was first revealed in a Top Secret Memorandum by a senior radio engineer with the Canadian Department of Transportation. Dated November 21,

1951, Smith wrote the following to the Controller of Telecommunications concerning flying saucer technologies being secretly studied in the U.S. by a very highly classified group:

    a. The matter is the most highly classified subject in the United States government, rating higher than the H-bomb,

    b. Flying saucers exist,

    c. Their modus operandi is unknown but a concentrated effort is being made by a small group headed by Dr. Vannevar Bush, and

    d. The entire matter is considered by the United States authorities to be of tremendous significance.[39]

Smith's memo confirms that a small group headed by Dr. Vannevar Bush was secretly studying the technologies associated with the UFO issue. Bush had earlier headed the Office of Scientific Research and Development (1941-1947) and the joint military services Research Development Board (RDB).[40] At the time of Smith's memo, Bush was on the oversight committee of the RDB and a leading scientific advisor to Truman.

Forrestal was certainly briefed about extraterrestrial life and technology during his tenure as Secretary of the Navy (1944-1947), and as the first Secretary of Defense (1947-1949). Later evidence to be presented will confirm this. Forrestal may have shared this information with John Kennedy whom the former hoped to recruit for his personal staff.

Was Forrestal Killed to Prevent Him Revealing the Truth about Extraterrestrial Life?

Significantly, James Forrestal died on May 22, 1949, under mysterious circumstances after being sacked by President Truman only two months earlier. Scholars argue Forrestal did not suffer a nervous breakdown, nor did he commit suicide as claimed in official records:

> Forrestal resigned because he was asked to resign by President Truman. He had not suffered a nervous breakdown. None of the doctors who treated him at Bethesda Naval Hospital described his condition as a nervous breakdown. What is more important, though, recently uncovered evidence greatly undermines the theory that Forrestal voluntarily jumped out of the window at Bethesda Naval Hospital. [41]

Evidence indicates Forrestal was forced to resign over some policy dispute, and was then committed to a medical facility to silence him. During his seven weeks at the Bethesda Naval Hospital, Forrestal was denied normal visitation rights. According to historian, Richard Dolan:

> Throughout Forrestal's hospitalization, access to him was severely restricted. One-time visitors were his wife, his two sons, Sidney Souers ... Louis Johnson, Truman, and Congressman Lyndon Johnson... Although Forrestal was presumably glad to see his sons, he was not close to any of these visitors, and had a political antipathy to his government colleagues who came by. However, Forrestal was not permitted to see the several people he continually asked to see: his brother, a friend, and two priests. [42]

After threats of going to the press and suing the hospital, Henry Forrestal was eventually able to visit his brother four times. The two priests and his personal friend, however, were denied access the entire time of Forrestal's "treatment." This was especially troubling to Henry Forrestal. The answer may have been that "a Catholic confessional might risk disclosing sensitive national security information." [43]

Curiously, one of the visitors to Forrestal's hospital suite was Congressman Lyndon Baines Johnson. According to one of Forrestal's aides, Marx Leva, Johnson "managed to gain entrance to the suite "against Forrestal's wishes."[44] This is a very significant revelation. It suggests Johnson was part of a group of public officials pressuring Forrestal to remain silent about something. When efforts to silence Forrest had failed, and he was about to be released into the custody of his brother, according to various sources, including his brother, Forrestal was murdered. Cornell Simpson writes:

> At his home in Beacon, New York, Henry Forrestal stated to this author that James Forrestal positively did not kill himself. He said his brother was the last person in the world who would have committed suicide and that he had no reason for taking his life. When Forrestal talked to his brother at the hospital, James was having a good time planning the things he would do following his discharge. Henry Forrestal recalled that Truman and [new Defense Secretary Louis] Johnson agreed that his brother was in fine shape and that the hospital officials admitted that he would have been released soon. To Henry Forrestal, the whole affair smelled to high heaven. He remarked about his brother's treatment at the hospital, his virtual imprisonment and the censorship of his visitors. Henry Forrestal had never heard of such treatment and questioned why it should have been allowed. He further questioned why the hospital officials lied about his brother being permitted all the visitors he wanted....He considered it odd that his brother had died just a few hours before he, Henry, was to arrive and take James out of the hospital. Then he repeated his belief that James

Forrestal did not kill himself; that he was murdered; that someone strangled him and threw him out the window.[45]

Dolan gives the following account of what happened when one of the two priests close to Forrestal finally arrived at the hospital:

> Father Sheehy had reason to suspect murder. When he arrived at Bethesda Naval Hospital after learning of Forrestal's death, an experienced-looking hospital corpsman approached him through the crowd. In a low, tense voice he said: "Father, you know Mr. Forrestal didn't kill himself, don't you?" Before Sheehy could respond or ask his name, others in the crowd pressed close, and the man quickly departed.[46]

What was it that Forrestal was telling others, likely including Kennedy, that may have resulted in his murder?

I will present evidence in subsequent chapters that Forrestal was a founding member of a control group set up to manage the UFO and extraterrestrial phenomenon in September 1947. As a key figure in a powerful group dictating UFO policy, Forrestal would have been expected to abide by majority decisions, even if he disagreed. If he did not, other members of the group would eventually view him as a threat to national security, and take whatever action they deemed necessary. Dolan's own conclusion after reviewing the circumstances of Forrestal's death was that it was related to some disagreement over UFO policy:

> An explanation centering on the UFO phenomenon accounts surprisingly well for the complete unhinging of a successful and brilliant individual, and more

importantly, the need to silence someone who could no longer be trusted.[47]

As a former journalist dedicated to the principles of a free press and open society, the indefinite cover up of such a momentous event as the discovery of extraterrestrial life was anathema to Forrestal's convictions. According to William Cooper, Forrestal wanted the truth to get out about UFOs, but he was overruled and forced to resign:

> He [Forrestal] was a very idealistic and religious man. He believed that the public should be told. James Forrestal was also one of the first known abductees. When he began to talk to leaders of the opposition party and leaders of the Congress about the alien problem he was asked to resign by Truman. He expressed his fears to many people. Rightfully, he believed that he was being watched. This was interpreted by those who were ignorant of the facts as paranoia. Forrestal later was said to have suffered a mental breakdown. He was ordered to the mental ward of Bethesda Naval Hospital. In spite of the fact that the Administration had no authority to have him committed, the order was carried out. In fact, it was feared that Forrestal would begin to talk again.[48]

If Forrestal wanted the truth to get out, then it would not be surprising that he would have briefed Kennedy either during their summer 1945 trip, or later.

In November, 1946, Kennedy was elected to the U.S. Congress. Kennedy and Forrestal were ideological allies and friends. If Forrestal indeed had his own extraterrestrial contact experiences, then it is likely he would have confided in Kennedy what had happened. This is especially the case if Forrestal was intent on releasing this information to the public. If this is an accurate account of his intentions, then we need to reconsider James Forrestal's legacy. He was a visionary who inspired Kennedy's own convictions about government transparency, freedom of the press and an open society. Ironically, Forrestal was a founding member of the most secretive organization in the National Security establishment – one that managed extraterrestrial affairs. It appears that he attempted to end the secrecy, but paid the ultimate price for doing so.

Apparently James Forrestal's 1949 death weighed heavily on Kennedy. Forrestal was the first senior public official to cultivate Kennedy, long before others had recognized Kennedy's potential. On their 1945 European tour, Forrestal introduced Kennedy to many powerful political and military leaders, including General Eisenhower. Kennedy was exposed to many secrets and classified government programs, possibly including Operation Paperclip. He may even have independently learned earlier of the interplanetary origins of the unknown aircraft recovered after the 1942 Los Angeles Air Raid. As a former Naval Intelligence officer, friend of Secretary Forrestal and possible staffer, Kennedy could be trusted to keep secrets.

On May 30, 1963, President Kennedy visited the grave of Secretary James Forrestal. The visit was highly significant. Why would a sitting President visit the grave of someone that had committed suicide, if we are to believe the official records? The visit came one week before Kennedy traveled to the contiguous military facilities at White Sands Missile Range, Holloman Air Force Base and Fort Bliss, which straddled the border between Texas and New Mexico.[49] He was met by Vice zPresident Johnson at El Paso, Texas. A local news report pointed out that "never before in the history of the Southwest have the President and vice president visited simultaneously."[50]

Figure 4. President Kennedy at the grave of James Forrestal, May 30, 1963. Source: JFK Presidential Library

White Sands was the home of former Nazi rocket scientists repatriated under Operation Paperclip. They were working on highly classified projects, some of which were alleged to involve extraterrestrial technologies recovered from different crash sites. If there was any truth to rumors about

29

classified military projects involving captured extraterrestrial technologies, Kennedy likely thought he could learn about them at these facilities.

From his 1945 visit to Germany, Kennedy learned about some of the advanced projects that Nazi German scientists had been working on. Now as President, he could visit the U.S. facilities where many of these scientists had been repatriated. It appeared that Kennedy's real purpose in visiting these military facilities was to learn firsthand about highly classified programs involving extraterrestrial technologies. This may have been why Vice President Johnson was also present.

Kennedy's visit to the grave of Forrestal was not merely to pay his respects to a former mentor who suffered a mental breakdown. Kennedy would have learned from Henry Forrestal, also a family friend, what he thought had happened to his brother. In subsequent chapters, I show that there is good reason to conclude that Kennedy believed Forrestal had been murdered for attempting to reveal the truth about alien life. If so, then Forrestal was the first senior U.S. official killed to maintain a cover-up of alien life.

At Forrestal's grave, a week before a highly significant visit to White Sands, Kennedy was speaking once more to an old friend. Perhaps Kennedy was silently telling him that he would use his authority as President to realize his friend's vision – a world where the existence of extraterrestrial life would be common knowledge. In following a similar path to Forrestal, Kennedy was resolved not to suffer the same fate.

Endnotes Chapter 1

---

[14] Robert Dallek, *An Unfinished Life : 1917-1963* (Hachette Book Group, 2013). Kindle Edition. 82 of 814

[15] John F. Kennedy, *Why England Slept* (Praeger, 1962)

[16] Robert Dallek, *An Unfinished Life : 1917-1963* (Hachette Book Group, 2013). Kindle Edition. 82 of 814

[17] Robert Dallek, *An Unfinished Life : 1917-1963*. Kindle Edition, 98 of 814

[18] Robert Dallek, *An Unfinished Life : 1917-1963*. Kindle Edition, 116-17 of 814

[19] *Prelude to Leadership: The Post-War Diary of John F. Kennedy* (Regency Publishing, 1995)

[20] *Prelude to Leadership: The Post-War Diary of John F. Kennedy*,71.

[21] *Prelude to Leadership: The Post-War Diary of John F. Kennedy*,102-103.

[22] *Prelude to Leadership: The Post-War Diary of John F. Kennedy*,104.

[23] Cited in *Prelude to Leadership: The Post-War Diary of John F. Kennedy*, 106

[24] See Wikipedia entry on "Operation Paperclip," http://en.wikipedia.org/wiki/Operation_Paperclip

[25] See http://www.archives.gov/iwg/declassified-records/rg-330-defense-secretary/

[26] Andrew Walker, "Project Paperclip: Dark side of the Moon," http://news.bbc.co.uk/2/hi/uk_news/magazine/4443934.stm

[27] For an overview of Nazi Germany's flying saucer technologies and the relationship to extraterrestrial life, see Michael Salla, "Foundations for Globally Managing Extraterrestrial Affairs – The Legacy of the Nazi Germany-Extraterrestrial Connection," http://exopolitics.org/Study-Paper-6.htm

[28] "Secrets of the Third Reich," http://www.bibliotecapleyades.net/ufo_aleman/esp_ufoaleman_8a.htm

[29] "Secrets of the Third Reich," http://www.bibliotecapleyades.net/ufo_aleman/esp_ufoaleman_8a.htm

[30] http://www.bibliotecapleyades.net/ciencia/ciencia_flyingobjects55.htm

[31] Available online at: http://majesticdocuments.com/pdf/marshall-fdr-march1942.pdf

[32] Linda Moulton Howe, "JFK, MJ-12 and Outer Space," http://presidentialufo.com/john-f-kennedy/73-president-kennedy-ufo-articles

[33] Available online at: http://majesticdocuments.com/pdf/marshall-fdr-march1942.pdf

[34] Document available online at: http://aboutfacts.net/ufo/UFO43/Small/HooverUFO.jpg

[35] John Kennedy, *Prelude to Leadership: The Post-War Diary of John F. Kennedy*,62-63.

[36] John Kennedy, *Prelude to Leadership: The Post-War Diary of John F. Kennedy*,65.

[37] John Kennedy, *Prelude to Leadership: The Post-War Diary of John F. Kennedy*,65-66.

[38] Linda Moulton Howe, "JFK, MJ-12 and Outer Space," http://presidentialufo.com/john-f-kennedy/73-president-kennedy-ufo-articles

[39] Smith's memo is available online at: http://www.majesticdocuments.com/pdf/smithmemo-21nov51.pdf

[40] Vannevar Bush's biography available online at: http://en.wikipedia.org/wiki/Vannevar_Bush

[41] David Martin, letter to former Virginia Governor, March 24, 2008: http://www.dcdave.com/article5/080429.htm

[42] Richard Dolan, "The Death of James Forrestal," http://rdolan.hostcentric.com/deathofjamesf.html

[43] Cited in David Martin, "Who Killed James Forrestal," http://www.dcdave.com/article4/021110.html

[44] Cited in David Martin, "Who Killed James Forrestal," http://www.dcdave.com/article4/021110.html

[45] Cited in David Martin, "Who Killed James Forrestal," http://www.dcdave.com/article4/021110.html Original Source: Cornel Simpson, *The Death of James Forrestal* (Western Islands Pub, 1966)

[46] Richard Dolan, "The Death of James Forrestal," http://rdolan.hostcentric.com/deathofjamesf.html

[47] Richard Dolan, "The Death of James Forrestal," http://rdolan.hostcentric.com/deathofjamesf.html

[48] See William Cooper, "The Secret Government: The Origin, Identity, and Purpose of MJ-12," http://www.bibliotecapleyades.net/sociopolitica/esp_sociopol_mj12_1.htm

[49] Source: http://elpasotimes.typepad.com/morgue/2013/04/1963-over-300000-will-greet-jfk-on-visit-to-el-paso.html

[50] Source: http://elpasotimes.typepad.com/morgue/2013/04/1963-over-300000-will-greet-jfk-on-visit-to-el-paso.html

Chapter 2

Eisenhower and Kennedy Receive Briefings on Roswell Flying Saucer Crash in 1947

Figure 5. First News Report on July 8, 1947

World Awakes to News of a Flying Saucer Crash at Roswell

On the morning of July 9, 1947, future Presidents Dwight D. Eisenhower and John F. Kennedy would awaken to news of conflicting reports that a flying saucer had crashed near the town of Roswell, New Mexico. According to the initial news reports, the flying saucer had crashed not far from the Roswell Army Air Field (AAF).[51] The Roswell AAF was at the time the home of the only operational nuclear bomber wing in the U.S., and the world. It had some of the most secure and highly trained personnel that the Army had to offer. It was the Army itself that authorized the first press release about the flying saucer crash. Briefly, the world was fixated with the news that we were not alone in the universe.

Then, as quickly as it was announced, the world was told that it was a big mistake. The army's highly trained intelligence staff had got it wrong. It was simply a weather balloon, and not an interplanetary flying saucer. Most of the world had a laugh at the expense of the Army's intelligence team, and that "military intelligence" must indeed be an oxymoron.

General Eisenhower and Congressman Kennedy were not laughing. Eisenhower was at the time the U.S. Army Chief of Staff and through formal Army channels knew the truth behind the conflicting newspaper reports. Kennedy was less than seven months into his first term as a U.S. Congressman, and through a more informal route using Congressional sources, also quickly learned the truth. The U.S. Army was covering up a momentous event - a flying saucer from another world had indeed crashed.

Flying Saucer Crash at Roswell

On the evening of July 2, 1947, a farmer by the name of Mack Brazel and others heard a loud explosion near his farm approximately 75 miles northwest of Roswell, in Lincoln County, New Mexico. On the morning of July 3, he investigated and found the wreckage of what appeared to be a flying saucer. On July 7, he reported the find to the Sheriff's office who notified the nearby Roswell Army Air Field (AAF) base that immediately sent two military intelligence officers to investigate. The result of the initial military investigation led to the famous press release on July 8 that a flying saucer had crashed. This generated instant media attention around the world. As the media interest began to build, another press release was quickly issued, this time by more senior military authorities, claiming the initial release was mistaken. It was only a weather balloon and not a flying saucer. Interest in the Roswell story then waned and it wasn't heard of again for another thirty years.

In 1978, one of the two military officers who conducted the initial investigation, Major Jesse Marcel, contacted Stanton Friedman, a veteran UFO researcher, and told him the truth about events at Roswell. According to Marcel, the crash debris "was nothing we had ever seen before."[52] It appeared indestructible, had strange hieroglyphic writing, and had other unearthly properties. He would state for the public record: "It was not an aircraft of any kind, that I am sure of. We didn't know what it was. It was nothing made on this Earth."[53]

Marcel took some of the debris home on the way to the base to show his wife and son. Jesse Marcel, Jr., eventually authored his own book about what he had had been shown by his father.[54] Marcel, Jr., a medical doctor with the U.S. Army who attained the rank of Colonel, agreed with his father that the Roswell wreckage "was nothing made on this Earth." If we can believe the testimony of father and son, a flying saucer had indeed crashed at Roswell, and Major Marcel had been ordered to take part in an official cover-up.

The subsequent publication of *The Roswell Incident* by Charles Berlitz and William Moore in 1980, which revealed the testimony of Marcel and other firsthand witnesses, brought the Roswell story back into public attention.[55] The 1947 Roswell Crash has ever since been on the center stage of public interest generating further investigations, official government/military reports, books and media interest.

In 2007, a book was published containing a notarized affidavit by another key military official involved in events at Roswell. Lieutenant Walter Haut became the Public Affairs Officer for Roswell Army Air Field in 1947. He was ordered to distribute the July 8 press release, claiming a flying saucer crash that led to world headlines. Haut's affidavit was written in December, 2002, and authorized for release after his death.[56] He died in December of 2005 and the affidavit was then published as the final chapter in the 2007 edition of a book by Thomas Carey and Donald Schmitt, *Witness to Roswell*.[57]

The affidavit has startling information about events occurring just before and after the Army's initial press release of a flying saucer crash. The significant event is that a staff meeting occurred on the morning of July 8, when Roswell AAF officers discussed how to deal with growing public and press interest in the wreckage found at TWO crash sites. Haut stated: "The main topic of discussion ... was an extensive debris field in Lincoln County approx. 75 miles NW of Roswell."[58] This was the crash site on Mack Brazel's farm that Major Marcel traveled to investigate on July 6 and 7. Marcel gave his report at the meeting. The second site was 40 miles north of Roswell, and was not generally known to researchers of the Roswell crash. The base commander, Col. William Blanchard, gave a brief report on wreckage found at the second site.

The most surprising fact about the staff meeting was that General Roger Ramey, whose headquarters was Carswell AAF Fort Worth, Texas, was also present. Haut reveals that Ramey devised a strategy for throwing the public and press off track about the two crash sites. According to Haut:

> One of the main concerns discussed at the meeting was whether we should go public or not with the discovery. General Ramey proposed a plan, which I believed **originated from his bosses at the Pentagon** [emphasis added]. Attention needed to be diverted from the more important site north of town by acknowledging the other location [Mack Brazel's ranch]. Too many civilians were already involved and the press already was informed.[59]

Ramey approved a press release pointing to the more remote and less important site near Mack Brazel's ranch. Haut wrote in his affidavit:

At approximately 9:30 am, Col Blanchard [Roswell AAF Base Commander] phoned my office and dictated the press release of having in our possession a flying disc, coming from a ranch northwest of Roswell, and Marcel flying the material to higher headquarters. I was to deliver the news release to radio stations KGFL and KSWE, and newspapers, the Daily Record and the Morning Dispatch.[60]

Later that afternoon, General Ramey retracted the "flying disc" announcement, replacing it with the weather balloon story that appeared in news reports on the evening of July 8 and the morning of July 9. This strategy succeeded in taking the flying saucer story off the news headlines, and confusing members of the public and press who had witnessed or were investigating events.

General Ramey's role in the cover up is significant. It was Ramey that ordered Major Jesse Marcel, whose report that a flying saucer had crashed at the more remote location in the July 8 press release, to fly to Fort Worth to appear at a press conference. Marcel was ordered to be photographed crouching quietly over what appeared to be material from a weather balloon. This was used to buttress Ramey's claim that the Roswell wreckage was really a misidentified weather balloon.

Major Marcel was forced to keep silent about the affair for over 30 years. It had been a humiliating experience for him. He was made to look foolish in having to publicly acquiesce to a retraction of his initial intelligence evaluation. After returning to Roswell Army Air Field, Marcel told Haut what had happened at Fort Worth:

Upon his return from Fort Worth, Major Marcel described to me taking pieces of the wreckage to Gen. Ramey's office and after returning from a map room,

37

finding the remains of a weather balloon and radar kite substituted while he was out of the room. Marcel was very upset over this situation. We would not discuss it again.[61]

Figure 6. Major Jesse Marcel crouches over weather balloon remains

Walter Haut claims in his affidavit that he was taken by the base commander, Col. Blanchard, to one of the Roswell hangars later on July 8 where he saw part of the wreckage that was relatively intact; it was about 15 feet long and 6 feet high.[62]

Haut also saw under canvas tarpaulin, with the heads sticking out, two bodies of the victims who appeared to be the size of a 10 year-old child. He said that at "a later date in Blanchard's office, he would extend his arm about 4 feet above the floor to indicate the height."[63]

Haut's affidavit indicates that Ramey was operating under orders by the Pentagon. It is clear that the staff meeting was focused on controlling press and public interest in the crash sites. No discussion occurred regarding supervising security at the two sites or retrieval of the crashed material from the second crash site 40 miles north of Roswell. Indeed, the only information released regarding the second crash site was that it had been witnessed by Col. Blanchard. It was not known to other Roswell Army Air Field officers prior to the July 8 staff meeting. It would have been expected that, given its proximity and resources, Roswell Army Air Field would play a prominent role in retrieval operations at the second site. This lack of involvement suggests that security and retrieval operations at the more sensitive "second crash site" were being supervised at a higher level than the general staff at Roswell Army Air Field. The most plausible explanation is that the Pentagon had deployed its own specialist teams for controlling security and retrieval operations at the more sensitive second site. Roswell Army Air Field would supply manpower, resources, and throw the public off the trail by issuing contradictory press releases. Evidence suggests that the investigatory team was a highly specialized covert team mentioned in a leaked classified document I will shortly discuss.

Overwhelming first hand witness testimony of events at Roswell, including the primary military officials involved in reporting and covering up key facts, strongly suggest that a flying saucer had indeed crashed. The earth was being visited by interplanetary visitors, and the Pentagon had ordered a cover-up at the highest levels. Who were Ramey's bosses at the

Pentagon that gave orders for the cover-up, and what was the name of the specialist recovery team? Leaked classified documents, while controversial, give plausible answers to these questions. They reveal that the most senior Pentagon official behind the cover-up was none other than five-star General, and Army Chief of Staff, Dwight D. Eisenhower.

General Eisenhower and Roswell Flying Saucer Crash

Eisenhower was appointed U.S. Army Chief of Staff on November 19, 1945, and oversaw the demobilization of millions of soldiers. As the Supreme Commander of Allied Forces in Europe and the first Governor of Occupied Germany, before returning to Washington in November 1945, he was deeply familiar with the covert effort to repatriate German scientists and technologies in Operation Paperclip.[64]

Two years after the end of hostilities in Europe, Eisenhower would certainly have been piqued by reports out of Roswell Army Air Field about a flying saucer crash. Did it involve covert Nazi technologies that the Army was developing? Or could the incident have involved a genuine interplanetary craft?

Leaked documents and witnesses reveal that Eisenhower played a leading role in decisions being made at the time about the UFO crash at Roswell. Two documents in particular reveal that he was among the first senior military officials to learn about the Roswell crash.

Eisenhower gave orders for Nathan Twining, the commanding general at the Air Material Command, Wright AAF (later renamed Wright-Patterson AFB), to travel to Alamogordo Army Air Field (later renamed Holloman AFB) and from there write a report of the Roswell crash. An almost identical Directive by President Truman suggests General Eisenhower was authorized by the President to play a leading role in the covert Army operation concerning the Roswell Crash.

Figure 7. General of the Army Dwight D. Eisenhower in 1947. Source: Eisenhower Presidential Library

The first document in question was a directive from General Eisenhower to General Nathan Twining on July 8 regarding the events at Roswell. Eisenhower ordered Twining to travel to White Sands Missile Base to "make an appraisal of the reported unidentified objects being kept there."[65] White Sands was where the former Nazi scientists, who were specialists in rocket technology, and therefore best able to evaluate the retrieved object, were located. Twining was also directed to "deal with the military, political and psychological situations, current and projected" surrounding the object."[66] In an almost identical directive to Twining, signed by President Truman on July 9, Truman asked that Twining "communicate with General Eisenhower to ascertain whether he desires you to proceed via Kirtland AAF."[67] Truman's directive outlined the leading role Eisenhower would take on the Roswell crash. In response to the Truman directive, one week later, Twining released an Air Accident Report to Army Air Force headquarters.[68] He reported that as far as aviation experts could determine, the disc was not created by the U.S. or any other country.

How legitimate are the Twining directives by Eisenhower and Truman, and the Air Accident Report by Twining? Dr. Robert Wood and his son Ryan, leading researchers of leaked documents allegedly dealing with extraterrestrial life and technologies, found sufficient evidence to conclude that the two directives and Air Accident Report are genuine.[69] Before discussing the legitimacy of these two allegedly "classified" documents, I want to introduce another allegedly "classified" document, a report about the Roswell crash that mentions an informal briefing received by Congressman Kennedy. The claimed briefing is important since it reveals that Kennedy learned about the Roswell crash, and this was known to restricted readership of the classified report. Significantly for what will be revealed later in this book, Eisenhower was aware that Kennedy had been briefed about the crash, for Eisenhower was among the readers of the report.

Interplanetary Phenomenon Unit Report and the Kennedy Briefing

John F. Kennedy had been elected in November, 1946, to the 11th Congressional district of the U.S. House of Representatives. His father, Joseph Kennedy, a wealthy businessman who had been the U.S. Ambassador to the United Kingdom (1937-1940), had high expectations for his sons. After the tragic death of his older brother, Joseph Jr., during World War II, John Fitzgerald had his father's high expectations pinned on him.

As a returned war hero with his father's wealth and influence backing his candidacy, Kennedy won his first election in a constituency dominated by working class Irish Americans. With his father's influence and networks, Kennedy was given sought-after committee assignments in his first Congressional term. These assignments would give him a platform for far more ambitious political goals later in his career. When on the morning of July 9, Kennedy awoke to newspaper reports of conflicting Army Press statements about the Roswell crash, he was in a position to use his Congressional resources and political networks to find out what had really happened.

With his Naval Intelligence background, Kennedy could immediately recognize something strange was happening with the conflicting press reports. Where there's smoke there's fire. One of three things may have happened.

Using his Congressional networks and military contacts, Kennedy could have made discreet inquiries, and taken into confidence by those in the loop regarding the events at Roswell.

**Figure 8. Official U.S Navy Portrait of Lt John F.
Kennedy. Source: JFK Presidential Library**

Alternatively, because powerful figures recognized that Kennedy was destined to advance far in Washington DC., someone may have decided to cultivate the freshman Congressman by briefing him about the most important event imaginable: an encounter with technologically evolved life from another planet. The most likely figure wanting to recruit Kennedy would have been Secretary of the Navy, James Forrestal. As mentioned earlier, he had tried unsuccessfully to recruit Kennedy for his personal staff in 1945. Did Forrestal now want to recruit Congressman Kennedy for another purpose?

The third possibility is that Kennedy was identified as someone who could be relied upon in Congress to assist in passing legislation supporting covert policies being developed on extraterrestrial life. His background in Naval Intelligence had exposed him to the importance of maintaining security oaths and classification. Kennedy knew how to keep a secret, and could play a valuable role in the unfolding cover-up of extraterrestrial life and technology.

Through confidential congressional and military sources, Kennedy could learn much more than was revealed to the public about the Roswell flying saucer incident, and why the Army had issued conflicting media releases. The key question that arises is, did Kennedy receive an informal briefing about the Roswell crash? According to an allegedly leaked military document, yes.

In a classified report by an elite Army counter intelligence team, Kennedy is mentioned as having received an informal briefing about the Roswell crash. The Counter Intelligence Corps[CIC]/Interplanetary Phenomenon Unit Report dated 22 July 1947, states:

> It has become known to CIC that some of the recovery operation was shared with Representative JOHN F. KENNEDY, Massachusetts Democrat elected to Congress in 46. Son of JOSEPH P. KENNEDY, Commission on Organization for the Executive Branch of the Government. KENNEDY had limited duty as naval officer assigned to Naval Intelligence during war. It is believed that information was obtained from source in Congress who is close to Secretary for Air Force.[70]

The reference to Kennedy is highly significant and revealing. The Interplanetary Phenomenon Unit report was intended for a very limited audience. It was a detailed summary of an investigation of what occurred at Roswell, as would have been expected if the original Army press release of an alien crash was correct. The Interplanetary Phenomenon Unit report states that Kennedy is a serving U.S. Congressman, the son of a highly influential politician, Joseph Kennedy, and served in U.S. Navy intelligence.

Basically, the report is telling its classified audience that Kennedy was someone who could be trusted to keep it all secret.

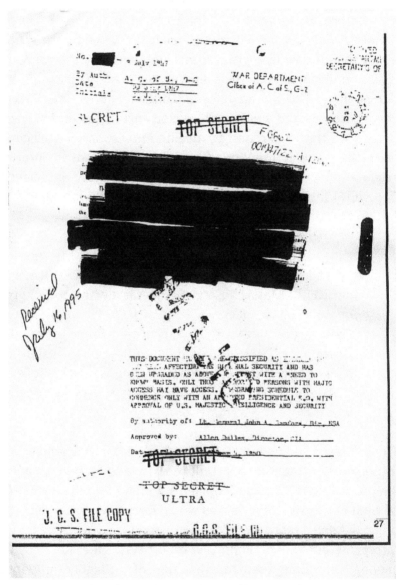

Figure 9. Cover Page showing IPU Report. Allegedly Reclassified in 1960. Source: Majestic Documents

Kennedy appeared to have been unofficially briefed about the Roswell UFO crash from an unnamed Congressional source close to the "Secretary for Air Force." At the time, Stuart Symington was Assistant Secretary of War for Air. Symington would become on September 18, 1947 the first Secretary for the newly formed U.S. Air Force. [71] In his official capacity, Symington would have certainly been informed about the UFO crash near Roswell Army Air Field.

Symington was a native of Massachusetts. According to credible sources, he was Kennedy's first choice as a running mate for the 1960 Presidential election, but was ultimately dropped in favor Lyndon Johnson. [72] It is possible that Symington's relationship with Kennedy began as a result of his arranging for Kennedy to receive an informal briefing that a flying saucer had indeed crashed and alien bodies recovered at the 1947 Roswell Crash. It is possible that Kennedy's support of Symington as his preferred Vice Presidential running mate was returning an important favor by Symington thirteen years earlier.

In the Interplanetary Phenomenon Unit Report, the Army Chief of Staff, General Eisenhower is also mentioned as one of the officials who would personally witness what was retrieved from Roswell along with the remains from another nearby crash site:

> On 7 July Lt General Nathan Twining arrived at Alamogordo AAF for a secret meeting with AAF Chief of Staff Spaatz and to view recovered remains of craft... It is believed that Twining and staff is preparing a detailed report of both incidents and briefings later to follow. It is also the belief of CIC that General Eisenhower will see a showing of recoveries sometime in late August this year. [73]

This passage is very revealing since it refers to the report that Twining was preparing in response to the Truman/Eisenhower directives. It also claims that Eisenhower would personally view what was retrieved at Roswell more than a month after the crash. Even though Eisenhower played a direct role in key decisions being made about the Roswell crash and its national security implications, he relied on subordinates such as Nathan Twining to brief him. Due to his busy schedule, commitments and impending retirement in February, 1948, Eisenhower was content to delegate responsibilities to army officers he could trust rather than viewing the material immediately. At the time of the Roswell incident, Eisenhower was already preparing to leave the U.S. Army.

The authenticity of the Interplanetary Phenomenon Unit Summary is disputed. Yet we do know that the Interplanetary Phenomenon Unit (IPU) was a highly classified army intelligence unit that did exist during the period in question. After initially denying its existence, the U.S. Air Force was eventually forced to acknowledge that the Interplanetary Phenomenon Unit did exist for a period of time. Documents released through the Freedom of Information Act (FOIA) confirmed the existence of this highly secretive investigatory group, despite the best efforts by Air Force officials to cast doubt on its existence.

In May 1984, UFO researcher William Steinman sent a FOIA request to the Army Directorate of Counterintelligence. Steinman received a reply from a Lieutenant Colonel Lance R. Cornine:

> As you note in your letter, the so-called Interplanetary Phenomenon Unit (IPU) was disestablished and, as far as we are aware, all records, if any, were transferred to the Air Force in the late 1950's. The 'unit' was formed as an in-house project purely as an interest item for the

Assistant Chief of Staff for Intelligence. It was never a 'unit' in the military sense, nor was it ever formally organized or reportable, it had no investigative function, mission or authority, and may not even have had any formal records at all. It is only through institutional memory that any recollection exists of this unit. We are therefore unable to answer your questions as to the exact purpose of the unit, exactly when it was disestablished, or who was in command. This last would not apply in any case, as no one was in 'command'. We have no records or documentation of any kind on this unit."[74]

Cornine's letter did acknowledge that the IPU did exist, but downplayed its existence as merely an "interest item" that was never an operational army "unit" of any kind.

Nearly three years later, in March, 1987, British researcher Timothy Good, also sent a FOIA request to the U.S. Army's Directorate of Intelligence. Good received a reply from Colonel William Guild. Guild's letter not only confirmed the IPU's existence but also revealed that the IPU was operational at one tim:.

Please be advised that the aforementioned Army unit was disestablished during the late 1950's and never reactivated. All records pertaining to this unit were surrendered to the U.S. Air Force Office of Special Investigations in conjunction with operation BLUEBOOK.[75]

So according to the Army's Directorate of Intelligence, the IPU did exist and was abolished in the late 1950s. No time line is given for when it was active.

According to a leaked military document cited earlier, the Interplanetary Phenomenon Unit was allegedly created in 1942 by orders of Army Chief of Staff, George Marshall, in response to the mysterious air raid over Los Angeles on February 24/25, 1942.[76] The Top Secret memo dated March 5, 1942 was addressed to President Roosevelt and explained how the Navy had recovered an "unidentified airplane" of "interplanetary origin." Marshall then ordered "Army G2" to create "a special intelligence unit" to "investigate the phenomenon."[77]

According to Dr. Robert Wood and his son Ryan:

> The memo bears correct Office of Chief of Staff (OCS) file numbers and has "Interplanetary Phenomenon Unit" (IPU) typed on it at a later time by a different typewriter. It is logical to believe that this is the order that sets up the IPU.[78]

While the Top Secret March 5, 1942, memo has not been confirmed by FOIA or the U.S. Army, it does give a plausible time line for the creation and function of the Interplanetary Phenomenon Unit. After its creation in 1942 as a unit within the Army's G-2 (Intelligence), we know that the Interplanetary Phenomenon Unit had been deactivated in the late 1950s by the Army's Directorate of Intelligence.

If the Marshall memo is genuine, the Interplanetary Phenomenon Unit had been a fully functional army unit tasked to investigate events concerning interplanetary phenomena since 1942. Even if the Interplanetary Phenomenon Unit was a real Army investigatory unit attached to the Army's Directorate of Intelligence, is its alleged Roswell crash report genuine? Did the Interplanetary Phenomenon Unit conduct a secret investigation in conjunction with the Army's Counter Intelligence Corps of events at Roswell?

The Haut Affidavit and the Interplanetary Phenomenon Unit Report

There are good reasons for concluding the Interplanetary Phenomenon Unit Report is genuine, and its reference to Kennedy being briefed about events at Roswell is accurate. We can examine some of Walter Haut's claims about the Roswell crash and the cover-up, and compare them to what the Interplanetary Phenomenon Unit Report said about the crash. It is worth emphasizing that the Interplanetary Phenomenon Unit Report was leaked to UFO researchers between 1993-1996, at least six years before Haut wrote his affidavit. There is high confidence among Roswell UFO researchers that Haut's testimony is a definitive account of key events that occurred during the Roswell crash. Therefore consistencies between the Interplanetary Phenomenon Unit Report and Haut's recollection of events, would be strong evidence that the (IPU) Report is a genuine government document.

Haut's affidavit reveals that the conflicting Army press releases were done to both distract from and cover-up a crash of an alien flying saucer at the second Roswell crash site. This is what the Interplanetary Phenomenon Unit had to say about the conflicting press reports and the second crash site (LZ-2):

> To maintain secrecy of site LZ-2, the CO of Roswell was authorized to give a brief press release to local paper in which 8th AF Hdqrs. promptly denied rumors that the Army had flying saucers in their possession which effectively killed press interest. [79]

This is consistent with the sequence of events described by Haut in his affidavit.

Also, the Interplanetary Phenomenon Unit Report refers to two crash sites. The first (LZ-1) was identified as the Mack

Brazel ranch. The second (LZ-2) is where, according to the IPU Report:

> ... the majority of structural detail of the craft's airframe, propulsion and navigation technology.... As to the bodies recovered at LZ-2, it appeared that none of the five crew members survived entry into our atmosphere due to unknown cause. [80]

Again, this is consistent with Haut's claims that the second site was more sensitive and the public/media had to be steered away by referring to LZ-1 in the initial press report. The Interplanetary Phenomenon Unit Report is also consistent with Haut's claim of seeing the remains of two alien bodies temporarily stored at the Roswell AAF.

Another reason is that the affidavit confirms that alien bodies had been retrieved at the second crash site which was closer to the town of Roswell. Jesse Marcel did not mention finding alien remains at the first crash site. It is therefore understandable why the Army would want to redirect media and public attention away from the LZ-2 crash site to the debris field at Mack Brazel's ranch. The latter was further away and more difficult to reach for independent confirmation. The wreckage at Mack Brazel's ranch could be more easily dismissed as a weather balloon. Again, there is an important consistency here between the Interplanetary Phenomenon Unit Report and the Haut affidavit.

A fourth reason is that the Interplanetary Phenomenon Unit Report's description of what was recovered from the first crash site, refers to the "recovery of five bodies in a damaged escape cylinder."[81] This is consistent with the claims Haut makes in his affidavit:

I was permitted from a safe distance to first observe the object just recovered north of town. It was approx. 12 to 15 feet in length, not quite as wide, about 6 feet high, and more of an egg shape…. Also from a distance, I was able to see a couple of bodies under a canvas tarpaulin. Only the heads extended beyond the covering, and I was not able to make out any features.[82]

It appears that debris from the two crash sites revealed an unsuccessful attempt by aliens to escape harm from an impending crash in an escape pod.

The consistencies between Haut's Affidavit and the IPU Report support the conclusion that the Interplanetary Phenomenon Unit Report is an authentic classified government document leaked to the public. One can surmise then that the Report's references to both General Eisenhower and Congressman Kennedy are substantially accurate.

Eisenhower and Kennedy were Briefed about the 1947 Roswell Crash

It is not a great surprise that General Eisenhower played a leading role in the appointment of, and orders given to, key officials to oversee the recovery of debris and bodies from the Roswell crash. Eisenhower was revered by both civilians and the military for his role in World War II, and was one of only two actively serving five star Army generals – the other being Douglas MacArthur. He was also Chief of Staff to the Department of War (Official name of the Army before the formation of the Department of Defense). It is therefore unthinkable that something as important as an interplanetary crash could occur near a major Army facility without Eisenhower being briefed. What is surprising is that Congressman John F. Kennedy also received a briefing.

As a freshman Congressman, Kennedy would not have been in a position to pursue what he may have learned informally through his sources about the Roswell crash. His initial interest and briefing regarding the flying saucer issue would have made clear to him that it was being handled at the highest classification level by the Truman administration and the national security system. Kennedy's friendship with Secretary Forrestal would have given him access to information that few others in Washington D.C. could hope to gain. Nevertheless, Kennedy would likely have realized the need to proceed cautiously despite his connections and family influence. It is reasonable to presume the congressional and military sources that had informally briefed Kennedy about Roswell, would have kept him apprised of how the extraterrestrial issue was being handled by the national security apparatus.

Kennedy would have concluded from his naval intelligence background, 1945 post-war Europe tour with Secretary Forrestal, and what he had been informally told, that a strict policy of secrecy was being maintained. The general public, the mass media, and many of Kennedy's congressional peers were being told that there was nothing to the flying saucer issue. From his own intelligence background and military connections, Kennedy likely realized that a psychological warfare program was underway to keep the flying saucer secret from breaking out. As Kennedy rose in seniority through the congressional ranks, he would be able to learn more about what he must have known was one of the most highly classified secrets in the USA.

In conclusion, firsthand whistleblower testimonies clarify many issues surrounding the Roswell crash. These testimonies help create a timeline of key events and personnel that can be used as a benchmark for validating the authenticity of allegedly leaked classified documents. In particular, the testimony of Walter Haut written in an affidavit published posthumously, helps corroborate many of the key events described in documents such as the Interplanetary Phenomenon Unit Report, and the Eisenhower and Twining directives. It is reasonable to conclude the information in these documents is an accurate summation of events as they took place back in 1947. Key among these events for the purposes of this book is that two future Presidents, General Eisenhower and Congressman Kennedy, were both briefed about the Roswell crash.

The whistleblower testimonies and leaked documents clearly demonstrate that out of concern for national security, a policy of deception was implemented. This deception involved senior national security officials from different branches of government including the then-Chief of Army Staff, General Eisenhower, President Truman; it continues to this day.

As a freshman Congressman from Massachusetts, Kennedy was certainly in no position to exercise a major influence on national security policy on extraterrestrial life. At best, Kennedy may have been able to influence Congressional legislation involving covert activities implemented by senior national security officials. If Kennedy learned about what really happened at Roswell, he would have to bide his time to have a chance to significantly influence national security policy on UFOs, and let the world know the truth about their extraterrestrial origins.

Kennedy's time would come 13 years later after he was elected President on November 8, 1960. He would privately meet President Eisenhower on several occasions to discuss transition issues between the incoming and outgoing administrations. Eisenhower would recall or be reminded that Kennedy had been briefed about the Roswell crash. It is reasonable to conclude that the highly classified topic of alien life would have been discussed. Especially so if President Eisenhower had anything important to share about how alien related projects were being covertly run in his administration.

55

It is probable General Eisenhower personally viewed the Roswell wreckage in late August, 1947, as mentioned in the Interplanetary Phenomenon Unit Report. Six months later, he would officially retire from Army life to become President of Columbia University. It would be five years later, after winning the 1952 Presidential election, that the Roswell crash and associated events would again demand Eisenhower's attention.

Endnotes Chapter 2

---

[51] The first report appeared in the Roswell Daily Record, July 8, 1947. Available online at: http://www.alien-earth.org/gallery/images/roswelldailyrecord.jpg

[52] Thomas Carey and Donald Schmitt, *Witness to Roswell: Unmasking the 60-Year Cover-up* (New Page Books, 2007) 81.

[53] Thomas Carey and Donald Schmitt, *Witness to Roswell: Unmasking the 60-Year Cover-up*, 81.

[54] Jesse Marcel Jnr, *The Roswell Legacy: The Untold Story of the First Military Officer at the 1947 Crash Site* (New Page Books, 2008). See also website: http://www.marceljr.com/

[55] Charles Berlitz and William Moore, *The Roswell Incident* (Grosset & Dunlop, 1980).

[56] http://roswellproof.homestead.com/haut.html#anchor_8

[57] Thomas Carey and Donald Schmitt, *Witness to Roswell: Unmasking the 60-Year Cover-up*. For a comprehensive book review, see David Rudiak, "Witness to Roswell," http://ufodigest.com/news/0607/witnesstoroswell.html

[58] Haut Affidavit #8, http://roswellproof.homestead.com/haut.html#anchor_8

[59] Haut Affidavit #9., http://roswellproof.homestead.com/haut.html#anchor_8

[60] Haut Affidavit #10., http://roswellproof.homestead.com/haut.html#anchor_8

[61] Haut Affidavit #16., http://roswellproof.homestead.com/haut.html#anchor_8

[62] Haut Affidavit #12., http://roswellproof.homestead.com/haut.html#anchor_8

[63] Haut Affidavit #13., http://roswellproof.homestead.com/haut.html#anchor_8

[64] See Wikipedia entry on "Operation Paperclip," http://en.wikipedia.org/wiki/Operation_Paperclip

[65] http://majesticdocuments.com/pdf/twining_eisenhower.pdf

[66] http://majesticdocuments.com/pdf/twining_eisenhower.pdf

[67] http://majesticdocuments.com/pdf/twining_truman.pdf

[68] Available online at: http://majesticdocuments.com/pdf/airaccidentreport.pdf

[69] In the Introduction to their compilation of Majestic Documents, the Woods team write: "Although we believe these documents are genuine, we are not including that evidence here since it will be presented in our upcoming book: THE SECRET: Evidence That We Are Not Alone," *The Majestic Documents* (Wood and Wood Enterprises, 1998).

[70] Counter-Intelligence Corps/Interplantery Phenonemon Unit Report, 6. Available online at: http://majesticdocuments.com/pdf/ipu_report.pdf

[71] Symington was Secretary of the USAF from September 18, 1947 to April 24, 1950. Biographical information at: http://en.wikipedia.org/wiki/Stuart_Symington

[72] See Wikipedia entry on Symington and the 1960 Presidential elections: http://en.wikipedia.org/wiki/Stuart_Symington

[73] Counter-Intelligence Corps/Interplantery Phenonemon Unit Report, 4. Available online at: http://majesticdocuments.com/pdf/ipu_report.pdf

[74] Available online at: http://www.textfiles.com/ufo/UFOBBS/1000/1723.ufo

[75] Timothy Good, *Above Top Secret*, p. 484.

[76] See Wikipedia entry for more info: http://en.wikipedia.org/wiki/Battle_of_Los_Angeles

[77] Available online at: http://majesticdocuments.com/pdf/marshall-fdr-march1942.pdf

[78] Robert and Ryan Wood, http://majesticdocuments.com/documents/pre1948.php

[79] IPU Report, 5. Available online at: http://majesticdocuments.com/pdf/ipu_report.pdf

[80] IPU Report, 2,6. Available online at: http://majesticdocuments.com/pdf/ipu_report.pdf

[81] Counter-Intelligence Corps/Interplantery Phenonemon Unit Report, 2. Available online at: http://majesticdocuments.com/pdf/ipu_report.pdf

[82] Haut Affidavit #12-13., http://roswellproof.homestead.com/haut.html#anchor_8

Chapter 3

President Eisenhower, MJ-12, S-4 and the Military Industrial Complex

Dwight Eisenhower's landslide win in the Presidential election of November 5, 1952, was not only a personal triumph, but also a return to power for the Republican Party. The Republicans had been out of the White House since the end of the Hoover administration on March 4, 1933. It was a long time in the political wilderness, but they had found their Moses to lead them to the Promised Land. The Republicans now had their man in the White House. The age of big government inaugurated by President Roosevelt was to be gradually turned back. Now corporate America would play a larger role in how the U.S. was run.

This was especially the case for how the U.S. was to manage its most sensitive national security projects. The influence and resources of major corporations took on a prominent role. Eisenhower turned to a scion of corporate America to restructure the U.S. bureaucracy, and its national security apparatus. Nelson Rockefeller, third son of American oil magnate John Rockefeller, was tasked by Eisenhower with restructuring the U.S. government. Among the things Rockefeller changed was how the office of the President was to manage the nation's biggest secret: the existence of extraterrestrial life and technology.

On November 18, 1952, two weeks after winning office, President-elect Eisenhower flew in to Washington D.C. to receive a number of classified briefings. One dealt with a secret which Wilbert Smith, a senior official in the Canadian government, described as more highly classified than the H-

59

Bomb.[83] The briefing dealt with select information about UFOs and extraterrestrial life.

The Eisenhower Briefing Document, an eight-page document leaked in 1984, has been closely examined by various UFO researchers.[84] Stanton Friedman, a former nuclear physicist, received grants from the Fund for UFO Research to study the Eisenhower Briefing document along with other allegedly leaked documents dealing with UFOs and extraterrestrial life. Friedman's task was to find out if the Eisenhower Briefing Document was genuine; or, as many suspected, a forged document designed to fool UFO researchers into chasing red herrings.

Friedman discovered, to his surprise, that many of the details in the Eisenhower Briefing were accurate. The dates, names and circumstances were consistent with the historical facts. For example, a key date was September 24, 1947, when President Truman signed a memo to the Secretary of Defense James Forrestal, authorizing the creation of "Operation Majestic Twelve." Truman stated that the program would be run by the President's Office after discussions between Forrestal, Dr. Vannevar Bush (Director of the Office of Scientific Research and Development) and the Director of Central Intelligence. Friedman discovered that in the seven month period between May and December, 1947, President Truman only met with Vannevar Bush once – on September 24.[85] Significantly, Bush was accompanied by Secretary Forrestal at the meeting. This was a stunning corroboration supporting the authenticity of both the Truman Memo and the Eisenhower Briefing Document that included the former as Appendix A.[86]

TOP SECRET
EYES ONLY
THE WHITE HOUSE
WASHINGTON

September 24, 1947.

MEMORANDUM FOR THE SECRETARY OF DEFENSE

Dear Secretary Forrestal:

As per our recent conversation on this matter, you are hereby authorized to proceed with all due speed and caution upon your undertaking. Hereafter this matter shall be referred to only as Operation Majestic Twelve.

It continues to be my feeling that any future considerations relative to the ultimate disposition of this matter should rest solely with the Office of the President following appropriate discussions with yourself, Dr. Bush and the Director of Central Intelligence.

Harry Truman

Friedman found there was no clear evidence to suggest that the Eisenhower Briefing Document and the Truman Memo were forged documents. In fact, there was good evidence to suggest the contrary, both appeared to be genuine. In his eventual book announcing the results of his research, he concluded: "Surprisingly, nothing that we had found or that others had alleged indicated that the documents were anything other than legitimate."[87]

The emergence of the Eisenhower Briefing Document in 1984 came four years after the publication a book written by William Moore and Charles Berlitz titled *The Roswell Incident*.[88]

61

It contained the stunning testimony of Jesse Marcel and other primary witnesses of the Roswell crash. For Friedman and other researchers fresh from learning about Roswell, the Eisenhower Briefing Document was the Rosetta Stone for understanding much of the UFO phenomenon.

The Eisenhower Briefing Document named the principle military and scientific figures involved with the UFO/extraterrestrial issue. It identified the main organization set up to manage the issue, the Majestic-12 (Majic-12 or MJ-12) Group comprising some of the most powerful figures in the U.S. national security apparatus. MJ-12 would report directly to the Office of the President:

> OPERATION MAJESTIC-12 is a TOP SECRET Research and Development/Intelligence operation responsible directly and only to the President of the United States. Operations of the project are carried out under the control of the Majestic-12 (Majic-12) Group which was established by special classified executive order of President Truman on 24 September, 1947, upon recommendation by Dr. Vannevar Bush and Secretary James Forrestal. (See Attachment "A".) Members of the Majestic-12 Group were designated as follows [see following figure]: [89]

Friedman's groundbreaking study of the Eisenhower Briefing Document uncovered a wealth of evidence that corroborated the existence of Majestic-12 (MJ-12) Group and its members.

TOP SECRET / MAJIC
EYES ONLY

002

• TOP SECRET •
••••••••••••••

COPY ONE OF ONE.

SUBJECT: OPERATION MAJESTIC-12 PRELIMINARY BRIEFING FOR
PRESIDENT-ELECT EISENHOWER.

DOCUMENT PREPARED 18 NOVEMBER, 1952.

BRIEFING OFFICER: ADM. ROSCOE H. HILLENKOETTER (MJ-1)

NOTE: This document has been prepared as a preliminary briefing
only. It should be regarded as introductory to a full operations
briefing intended to follow.

• • • • • •

OPERATION MAJESTIC-12 is a TOP SECRET Research and Development/
Intelligence operation responsible directly and only to the
President of the United States. Operations of the project are
carried out under control of the Majestic-12 (Majic-12) Group
which was established by special classified executive order of
President Truman on 24 September, 1947, upon recommendation by
Dr. Vannevar Bush and Secretary James Forrestal. (See Attachment
"A".) Members of the Majestic-12 Group were designated as follows:

Adm. Roscoe H. Hillenkoetter
Dr. Vannevar Bush
Secy. James V. Forrestal*
Gen. Nathan F. Twining
Gen. Hoyt S. Vandenberg
Dr. Detlev Bronk
Dr. Jerome Hunsaker
Mr. Sidney W. Souers
Mr. Gordon Gray
Dr. Donald Menzel
Gen. Robert M. Montague
Dr. Lloyd V. Berkner

The death of Secretary Forrestal on 22 May, 1949, created
a vacancy which remained unfilled until 01 August, 1950, upon
which date Gen. Walter B. Smith was designated as permanent
replacement.

••••••••••••••
• TOP SECRET •

TOP SECRET / MAJIC

EYES ONLY

EYES ONLY

T52-EXEMPT (E)

002

Figure 11. Eisenhower Briefing Document, p. 2. Majestic Documents

Majestic-12 Group (1947-1949)

MJ-1. Adm Roscoe Hillenkoetter — MJ-2. Dr. Vannevar Bush — MJ-3. Sec. James Forrestal

MJ-4. Gen. Nathan Twining — MJ-5. Gen. Hoyt Vandenberg — MJ-6. Dr. Detlev Bronk

MJ-7. Dr. Jerome Hunsaker — MJ-8. Adm. Sidney Souers — MJ-9. Gordon Gray

MJ-10. Dr. Donald Menzel — MJ-11. Gen. Robert Montague — MJ-12. Dr Lloyd Berkner

Figure 12. Initial Members of Majestic-12 Group

As far as the names are concerned, Friedman found that the twelve figures involved were eminently suited for a committee that would run the entire UFO/extraterrestrial phenomenon. Interestingly, the Eisenhower Briefing was released only three months after the last surviving member of the group, Dr. Jerome Hunsaker, had died – September 10, 1984. This hints at some prior agreement over the public release of such information.

The members of the MJ-12 Group represented a cross-section of the military, scientific and intelligence communities. After conducting a detailed analysis of each of those named in the Eisenhower Briefing Document, Friedman concluded:

> There were close links within this group of very important people. Considering what was happening in America and around the world post-World War II, they were a natural group to be on a committee such as Majestic-12. Either by aptitude, position, or geographic location, their inclusion would be fairly obvious.[90]

The head of Majestic-12 Group was the Director of Central Intelligence, Admiral Roscoe Hillenkoetter. This is important to keep in mind as we uncover evidence of the leading role the CIA would play in the future with Operation Majestic-12.

Official Government Documents Supporting the Existence of the Majestic-12 Group

Friedman eventually found startling corroboration for the existence of Majestic-12: a document sitting in the National Archives called the Cutler-Twining Memo, issued on July 14, 1954. It was a Top Secret memorandum for General Nathan Twining (a member of MJ-12) from Robert Cutler who was a Special Assistant to President Eisenhower. The memo stated:

The President has decided that the MJ-12 SSP briefing should take place during the already scheduled White House meeting of July 16, rather than following it as previously intended.[91]

The subject line of the Memorandum states "NSC/MJ-12 Special Studies Project." Unlike other Majestic documents, the Cutler Twining Memo was an official government document housed at the National Archives that had been declassified from Top Secret. It was found among a group of declassified Air Force documents and copied by the archivist, Ed Reese, as part of official records belonging to the National Archives.[92] The "Cutler-Twining Memo" is among the most authoritative documentary sources so far to prove the existence of an MJ-12 Special Studies Project.[93] Friedman succeeded in finding a government document that corroborated one of the key facts revealed by the Eisenhower Briefing Document: a secret organization that dealt with highly sensitive national security information existed, and its name was Majestic-12.

There is further official documentation supporting the existence of a highly classified control group dealing with UFOs/flying saucers. In chapter 2, I mentioned the Top Secret memo from Wilbert Smith to the Canadian Department of Transportation on November 21, 1951. Smith had officially reported to the Controller of Telecommunications concerning flying saucer technologies being secretly studied in the U.S. "by a small group headed by Dr. Vannevar Bush."[94]

Smith's memo confirms that, in 1951, a small group headed by Dr Vannevar Bush was secretly studying the technologies associated with the UFO issue. Bush had earlier headed the Office of Scientific Research and Development (1941-1947), and the joint military services Research Development Board (RDB).[95] At the time of Smith's memo, Bush

July 14, 1954

MEMORANDUM FOR GENERAL TWINING

SUBJECT: NSC/MJ-12 Special Studies Project

The President has decided that the MJ-12 SSP briefing should take place during the already scheduled White House meeting of July 16, rather than following it as previously intended. More precise arrangements will be explained to you upon arrival. Please alter your plans accordingly.

Your concurrence in the above change of arrangements is assumed.

ROBERT CUTLER
Special Assistant
to the President

was on the oversight committee of the RDB and a leading scientific advisor to Truman.

The final documentation to prove the existence of a highly classified project called Majestic-12 involves three 1952 Top Secret memos from the Joint Chiefs of Staff titled: "Joint Logistic Plan for MAJESTIC." The memos were declassified in 1976 and state:

The following plans in support of MAJESTIC are now under preparation: A psychological warfare plan, an unconventional warfare plan, cover and deception plans, a civil affairs/military government plan, a command plan, a logistic plan, transportation guidance, to be included in the logistic plan, a map and chart plan and a communications plan." [96]

These memos show that in 1952, a project called Majestic was underway and this involved significant support across a wide spectrum of issues, as would be expected for something involving UFOs and extraterrestrial life. The Joint Chiefs' memos corroborate the 1954 Cutler Twining Memo, and Smith's memo referring to a small group headed by Vannevar Bush.

Taken collectively, the Cutler-Twining Memo, the Smith Memo, and the Joint Chiefs of Staff Memos conclusively show that a Top Secret military scientific group responsible for dealing with extraterrestrial life and technology called at the time – Majestic-12 Group, Special Studies Project, or some variation, did, in fact, exist. These documents reveal that MJ-12 operated in a highly classified manner on the subject of flying saucers; worked within the NSC system implemented by President Truman; and was given enormous logistical support by the Pentagon. These official government documents authenticate the Eisenhower Briefing Document and the Truman Memo.

Eisenhower's Response to his Classified UFO Briefing

We have no historical record of the President-elect's response to the briefing described in the Eisenhower Briefing Document. As a former five-star general, Supreme Commander of Allied Forces in Europe, and Army Chief of Staff, Eisenhower would predictably have received briefings when key historic incidents in the document had occurred. In particular, as Army Chief of Staff (1945-1948) at the time of the 1947 Roswell UFO incident, Eisenhower would have been intimately familiar with the circumstances of the crash and the national security reasons for the cover-up. As discussed in the previous chapter, not only was Eisenhower briefed, but he played in a key role in the appointment of officials and events that culminated in the cover-up of the Roswell crash.

By November 1952, however, Eisenhower had been out of the military for six months and was serving full-time as President of Columbia University. The events and circumstances detailed in the Eisenhower Briefing Document required long-term thinking on the part of the incoming President. Eisenhower knew that the key to any successful military operation was to conduct a strategic study of one's resources, personnel and capabilities in order to meet future contingencies. The U.S. government had a vast bureaucracy and had to deal with the ultimate national security contingency in total secrecy – the existence of technologically developed visitors from other worlds. Eisenhower was to appoint a trusted figure to come up with a strategic plan for how to best reorganize the U.S. bureaucracy to meet future contingencies. That man was Nelson Rockefeller.

On January 24, 1953, by Executive Order (10432), President Eisenhower established the "Advisory Committee on Government Organization" whose primary goal was to reorganize the U.S. Federal government.[97] Eisenhower nominated Nelson Rockefeller to chair the committee that would directly report to the President with its recommendations for final approval. Rockefeller was chairman from 1953-59, and was therefore the person to whom the President would turn for the Committee's recommendations on how best to reorganize the U.S. government. After Rockefeller passed on the Committee's recommendations, they would be implemented by different federal departments and agencies in the manner Eisenhower decided was most appropriate. As Chairman of the Committee, Rockefeller was in a position to greatly influence the final recommendations that would be put to President Eisenhower, and how these could be implemented.

Among the recommendations that Rockefeller passed on to Eisenhower was how to reorganize the national security apparatus to accommodate the activities and goals of MJ-12. Rockefeller's final recommendation was to more deeply hide the Majestic-12 committee in the shadowy world of covert operations - a world in which he now played a key role on behalf of the Eisenhower administration.

In addition to his role in chairing the President's Advisory Committee on Government Organization, in 1954 Rockefeller was appointed Special Assistant for Cold War Planning by Eisenhower. The latter position officially involved the "monitoring and approval of covert CIA operations."[98] Rockefeller therefore worked directly with the covert operations division of the CIA – the "Directorate of Plans" - that was then headed by Frank Wisner. In January, 1959, the Directorate of Plans would be taken over by Richard Bissell who, we will see, was instrumental in the acquisition and development of Area 51 in 1955. In working with the CIA's "Black Operations," Rockefeller found a suitable vehicle through which the Majestic-12 (MJ-12) Group could conduct its business in complete secrecy without interference from ambitious politicians; or, ultimately, as we will see, President Eisenhower himself.

Rockefeller ensured that MJ-12 would now have greater autonomy from the Office of the President in order to immunize MJ-12 and the classified projects it ran from the uncertainties of the American political process. It made little sense to subject U.S. national security, in its ultimate quest to develop a long-term strategic answer to extraterrestrial visitors, to the short-term contingencies of politicians periodically consumed with the need to be re-elected. MJ-12 had to have its autonomy. This required removing it from direct oversight by the office of the President; so went the argument. Eisenhower, to his ultimate regret, would agree with this flawed argument put to him in one of Rockefeller's recommendations for government reorganization.

Under the Eisenhower administration, a major base of MJ-12 operations was Wright-Patterson Air Force Base. Wright-Patterson (previous called Wright Army Air Field) was the location where the 1947 Roswell crash material was taken for study. The remains of other UFO crashes, as mentioned in the Eisenhower Briefing Document would also be taken to Wright-Patterson.

Covert operations out of Wright-Patterson AFB offered both advantages and disadvantages for MJ-12. A key advantage was that some of the world's best aviation engineers worked out of Wright-Patterson. They were more than capable of reverse engineering advanced technologies retrieved from foreign powers – as they had done during World War II with captured Nazi jet fighters. MJ-12 meetings at Wright-Patterson offered the opportunity to directly study the technologies and entities recovered from crashes with the Air Force's top engineers and scientists. A little known non-governmental agency called the Battelle Institute, situated near Wright-Patterson AFB, would offer a suitable venue for MJ-12 meetings.[99] The major disadvantage of Wright-Patterson was that it was an Air Force Installation firmly under the control of Pentagon, and ultimately the President.

Where would MJ-12 establish its ultimate base of operations, away from the prying eyes of the Presidency, and from the military services that competed for control over various aspects of the UFO/extraterrestrial phenomenon? It would be a remote part of the Nevada desert owned at the time by the Department of Energy.

71

The CIA and Area 51

A CIA document that was declassified and released on June 25, 2013 confirms that in 1955 a remote section of the Nevada testing facility was handed over to the control of the CIA. Titled *The Central Intelligence Agency and Overhead Reconnaissance: The U-2 and Oxcart Programs, 1954-1974*, the document for the first time officially acknowledged the existence of Area 51.[100] According to the CIA document, Area 51 was ideal for the development and testing of secret spy planes that could be used against the Soviet Union. The area was adjacent to a dry desert bed called Groom Lake where an unusually long runway could be built along with the necessary underground research and development facilities. Richard Bissell, then working under Frank Wisner in the CIA's covert operations division, was put in charge of the acquisition of Area 51:

> On 12 April 1955 Richard Bissell and Col. Osmund Ritland (the senior Air Force officer on the project staff) flew over Nevada with Kelly Johnson in a small Beechcraft plane piloted by Lockheed's chief test pilot, Tony LeVier. They spotted what appeared to be an airstrip by a salt flat known as Groom Lake, near the northeast corner of the Atomic Energy Commission's (AEC) Nevada Proving Ground.... Bissell and his colleagues all agreed that Groom Lake would make an ideal site for testing the U-2 and training its pilots.[101]

The CIA's acquisition of Area 51 from the Department of Energy was signed off by President Eisenhower himself. [102] Over the next decades, some of the most advanced aviation programs would be developed at the facility built near Groom Lake at Area 51 with the assistance of aeronautical companies such as

Lockheed. According to the declassified document, the CIA would have ultimate responsibility for ensuring security at Area 51:

> On 29 April 1955, Richard Bissell signed an agreement with the Air Force and the Navy (which at that time was also interested in the U-2) in which the services agreed that the CIA "assumed primary responsibility for all security" for the overhead reconnaissance project (AQUATONE). From this time on, the CIA has been responsible for the security of overhead programs.[103]

This is worth emphasizing since it means that whatever facilities were built at Area 51, it would be the CIA that had "primary responsibility" over who gained access, or was given a briefing. Neither the U.S. Air Force nor the Navy, would ultimately be in control of the classified projects happening at Area 51. It would be the CIA. This is surprising given that the military services had vast resources and a history in handling advanced technologies acquired by the US. As mentioned earlier, Nazi jet fighters and other advanced weapons were taken to military facilities such as Wright Army Air Field (aka Wright-Patterson AFB) for study and reverse engineering during World War II. The CIA was a brand-new government agency created only in 1947. Clearly, the Majestic-12 group believed the CIA offered important advantages among which was that it would certainly pose fewer institutional obstacles to how MJ-12 wanted to run its projects.

The CIA's Directorate of Plans (covert operations) headed by Frank Wisner (1951-1958) and later Richard Bissell (1959-1962) would play critical roles in the future security of Area 51 facilities. More important would be their respective roles in acquiring extraterrestrial technologies found anywhere in the world for final relocation to Area 51. This would require great coordination and cooperation among different military and intelligence services around the world. While the Directorate of Plans would have the personnel and resources to covertly relocate extraterrestrial technologies, it would be up the CIA's Counterintelligence Division to ensure this was done without any leaks.

It was the Counterintelligence Division's job to monitor CIA spies and covert operatives to ensure they had not been compromised by foreign intelligence agencies. The CIA CI division was run by James Jesus Angleton from 1954 to 1975. Angleton was a protégé of then serving CIA Director Allen Dulles (1953-1961), who, it will be later revealed, also headed MJ-12 at the time Area 51 became operational. It appears that the Majestic-12 Group had adopted a protocol that the serving CIA director would be appointed to head MJ-12.

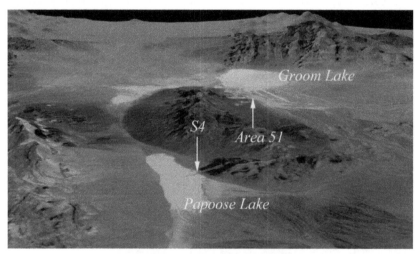

Figure 14. Area 51 with S-4 facility

What the declassified CIA document does not mention is the building of a second, even more highly classified, facility at Area 51. This second facility was built next to Papoose Lake, on the southern side of the Papoose Mountain range, approximately 10 miles south-west of Groom Lake.

It is worth repeating that it would be the CIA (more specifically, its Directorate of Plans and Counterintelligence divisions) that was in charge of security for this even more secretive facility at Papoose Lake. This second facility was to be MJ-12's ultimate base of operations, and MJ-12 would use the CIA as its proxy for controlling what would be called "S-4".

Whistleblower Testimonies about S-4

Information about the S-4 facility has been revealed by a number of whistleblowers. While controversy surrounds each of the whistleblowers concerning documentation to substantiate their testimonies, to date these are the only eyewitness accounts of the mysterious S-4 facility. Space does not allow an exhaustive analysis of their credibility as witnesses, and the controversy surrounding each. It's worth pointing out that it is illegal to reveal information or documents about a classified U.S. facility or program that has not been acknowledged to officially exist. Here is how the Pentagon describes Unacknowledged Special Access Programs (SAPs):

> Unacknowledged SAPs require a significantly greater degree of protection than acknowledged SAPs... A SAP with protective controls that ensures the existence of the Program is not acknowledged, affirmed, or made known to any person not authorized for such information. All aspects (e.g., technical, operational, logistical, etc.) are handled in an unacknowledged manner.[104]

It could be expected that there would be little, if any, official documentation that could be found to substantiate whistleblower claims of working at such a classified facility. Consequently, I will briefly summarize each of their testimonies and give references for the reader to further research their claims and the controversy over their credibility.

The first and most famous of the whistleblowers is Robert Lazar who, in November 1989, went public with his experiences at the highly classified S-4 facility. Lazar described a facility housing nine different flying saucer-type craft using incredibly advanced propulsion and navigation technologies. He was asked to participate in an attempt to reverse engineer one of the propulsion systems. Lazar claims that the advanced vehicles were regularly tested on a particular night and hour. Sure enough, at the scheduled time, Lazar and several associates witnessed the flying saucer craft being tested over Area 51. One of the propulsion systems identified by Lazar involved the breaking apart of a stable isotope of Element 115, in a manner that generated anti-matter which could then be used to power the spacecraft. Lazar even claims that he briefly sighted an extraterrestrial at S-4, suggesting that the Papoose Lake facility handled both extraterrestrial life and technologies.

While Lazar's testimony has been hotly debated, recent scientific advances lend credibility to his claims.[105] For example, it has been confirmed that element 115 does exist, and was added to the periodic table as Unumpentium.[106] Also, Lazar took several UFO researchers and a Japanese film crew to monitor secret testing of the flying saucer technologies from vantage points on State Route 375 (renamed Extraterrestrial Highway in 1996) adjacent to Area 51.[107] The craft were witnessed and captured on film, confirming Lazar's direct knowledge of the testing schedule of craft out of Area 51.

Two years after Lazar introduced the world to Area 51 and S-4, Derek Hennessy (aka Connor O'Ryan) approached famed UFO researcher Wendelle Stevens (Lt Col, USAF ret.) with his own S-4 story in 1991.[108] Hennessy claims to have been a former Navy Seal recruited to work in the classified world of UFO/extraterrestrial projects based at S-4. He said that part of his work involved the assassination of individuals who were deemed by MJ-12 to be national security threats. During the cooling down period after his "assignments", he would be taken to S-4 to work as a security guard before being given a new assignment. He says he witnessed VIPs such as then Defense Secretary Dick Cheney visit the S-4 facility and directly observe the different space craft and alien bodies.[109] Eventually, Hennessy attempted to leave the program when he suspected he was himself targeted for elimination. After he contacted Stevens in 1991, he went for a short period into hiding at a remote location provided by Stevens. Hennessy gave extensive interviews to Stevens and other UFO researchers, and recorded six hours of video testimony of his work for MJ-12 and what he saw at S-4.[110]

Another S-4 whistleblower was Steve Wilson who claimed to be a retired Air Force Lt. Colonel who worked on a highly classified program called "Project Pounce." This was allegedly an inter-services program aimed at locating, securing and retrieving downed UFOs from around the world. According to Wilson, alien crafts would be taken to S-4 for further study, not the Groom Lake facility! This is how he described his first visit to S-4, according to UFO researcher Dr. Richard Boylan:

> The plane circled and set down on a dry lake bed. Later he learned it was Papoose Dry Lake [S-4], deep within the Nellis Air Force Range in central Nevada. Even up close, the mountains and terrain looked barren. They walked about 300 yards to a rock outcropping. On the other side, nestled between some large rocks, was an iron door with no handle. The scruffy-looking CIA man somehow opened the door. They went inside and down a tunnel. At the end of the passageway, Wilson glanced around quickly. He still marvels at the size of the structure. "I could swear that the whole damned mountain was hollow. Right down the middle was a runway, and at the

end huge doors, that I later found could be opened to allow a plane to take off right out of the mountain." [111]

Significantly, Wilson's account corroborates the declassified CIA document that it is the CIA that provides security at Area 51. Wilson claims to have witnessed eight flying saucer craft at S-4, and personally met an eight-foot tall blond extraterrestrial female giving employees a galactic history lesson. [112] Wilson retired in 1980; in 1995 he decided to become a whistleblower and reveal what he knew. In 1997, he died from a particularly malicious form of cancer that raised suspicions that he had been targeted and silenced for his recent revelations. [113]

Dan Burisch claims to have a doctorate in microbiology and was first recruited by MJ-12 in 1986 while still a student. [114] He says that upon his return from the 1991 Iraq War where he worked on countering biological warfare agents that might be used, he began his classified work at S-4. He described being assigned to work directly with an extraterrestrial being (J-Rod) held on the fifth level of the S-4 facility in a "clean sphere" environment. [115] He says that the extraterrestrial did a mind-meld with him and transferred much information about its civilization, their history and activities on Earth. He identified two distinct groups of Gray extraterrestrials interacting with humanity aiming to regenerate their species with human genetics, and a Nordic-looking group of extraterrestrials from the Orion constellation more interested in promoting spiritual awareness. Burisch claimed that he worked on Project Lotus, a top secret program focusing on the generation of life. He says that he also worked on Project Looking Glass, a device that was used for bending time and space in ways that could allow looking into the future. Burisch says he worked directly with MJ-12, the leader (MJ-1) of which at the time was Admiral Mike McConnell. Burisch even claims to have personally served on the MJ-12 Group for a short period as a pro-tem member in 2005.

In 1997, an anonymous whistleblower calling himself "Victor" came forward to reveal what he knew about a captured alien held at the remote S-4 facility located on Area 51.[116] What made Victor different was that he had a video to prove what he was saying was real.[117] The video itself takes place in a darkened room where a large-headed creature with big black eyes appearing like a classic Gray alien is being interviewed by two individuals. One is allegedly a general asking questions while the other is a telepathic communicator relaying the alien's responses. Towards the end of the nearly three minute video segment, the Gray alien being appears to have breathing difficulties and is helped by two medics who rush into the room to give assistance.

Figure 15. Screen Shot from Alien Interview Video

The Alien Interview video has been controversial since it was first aired in 1997 in a documentary titled: *Area 51: The Alien Interview.*[118] UFO researchers, however, have gone on the record in support of the video's authenticity. Jim Dilettoso, a highly respected image analyst evaluated the video frame by frame and did not find any evidence of fraud. Victor's testimony and video appears to be yet another piece of evidence that S-4 is the secure military facility where live extraterrestrials are taken for questioning by authorized officials.

Finally, we have the case of Michael Kruvant Wolf who also claims to have worked at S-4 and to have served on the MJ-12 Group. Wolf was born in 1942 and enjoyed a normal childhood until he had an extraterrestrial contact experience, after which his intellectual interests and abilities expanded rapidly. At age 12 he started his own UFO club, the "Flying Saucer Research Association of New Jersey," and developed contact protocols using light rays for interacting with extraterrestrial craft. He attracted the interest of veteran UFO researchers such as George Hunt Williamson who wrote about the success of the young Wolf's contact protocols in *Road In The Sky*.[119] Wolf impressed Williamson by getting a UFO to fly overhead in a specified direction. While still in high school, the precocious Wolf claims he was recruited by Majestic-12 which subsequently paid for his education.

Wolf gave various interviews to UFO researchers and wrote about his experiences in a book titled *Catchers of Heaven*.[120] Briefly, he claims to have worked with extraterrestrials at S-4 on various technology and bioengineering projects.[121] Wolf pioneered advanced cloning technologies in a super-soldier program that produced the first human clone, "J-Type Omega," partly based on Wolf's own genetic material. He says that he also pioneered the Gateway treatment that would "open the brain up – a way to stimulate the neurons allowing billions of synapses to form and therefore use of a vast increased mind."[122]

Wolf even claims to have given shelter to an injured Gray alien called Kolta who visited Wolf at his apartment. Confirmation for his incredible claim came in an interview of French aristocrat Philippe de la Messuziere, who visited Wolf at his Connecticut apartment and witnessed the live alien, Kolta.[123] Messuziere claims to have even photographed Kolta.

Wolf spoke regularly with leading scientists, including Dr. Hal Puthoff, who consulted him on a number of technical issues.[124] Another whistleblower went on the public record about his conversations with Wolf. Edgar Fouche worked at Area 51 as an electronics specialist, and was familiar with many top secret programs there.[125] Fouche wrote:

> I talked on the phone many times to Michael Wolf Kruvant … We talked up until he died… The strange thing is that when I questioned Michael over the phone, he would always answer correctly when I asked about military programs/projects, who was in charge of them, etc. I mostly asked him things only me and my friends knew. So if he was lying then he was brilliant at it.[126]

Most significantly, Wolf told UFO researchers that he was particularly close to James Jesus Angleton who, evidently, was involved in his initial recruitment and took on a mentoring role for the young Wolf.[127] An Italian Intelligence agent confidentially confirmed to a UFO researcher that Angleton had indeed mentored Wolf.[128] This is the first direct reference to the CIA's counterintelligence chief playing a leading role in projects and interacting with personnel at S-4. It appears that he led a covert program to recruit young prodigies with abilities relevant to the study of extraterrestrial life. We will see in later chapters that Angleton was closely involved in the surveillance of individuals with classified UFO information, and was the CIA's gatekeeper on the extraterrestrial issue.

CIA and S-4 Facility at Area 51

The S-4 facility, physically located at Area 51, was designed to be run as a state-within-a-state. With the CIA assuming "primary responsibility for all security", it meant that the Director of the CIA would provide funds for S-4 projects and resources using the CIA's unique statutory authority to create a "black budget" that circumscribed Congressional oversight. The CIA has the unique legal ability among all U.S. government departments and agencies to generate funds through appropriations of federal government agencies and other sources "without regard to any provisions of law" and without regard to the intent behind Congressional appropriations. [129] This would mean that vast funds could be made available without the U.S. Congress monitoring or auditing the CIA. As with Area 51 where two facilities were created, with one (the official Area 51 facility at Groom Lake) giving cover for the other more secretive facility (S-4 at Papoose Lake), there would be two black budgets created by the CIA.

The size of the "official" black budget was revealed by the CIA in 1997 to be almost $27 billion for the entire intelligence community. [130] By 2013, the black budget had grown to $53 billion. The "official" black budget was designed to be distributed to the different intelligence agencies including the CIA. In August 2013, Edward Snowden leaked NSA documents showing how the "official" black budget of $53 billion was apportioned to the intelligence community, including the CIA. [131] Funds from the "official" black budget are how the CIA funded its publically acknowledged spy plane projects out of the Groom Lake facility at Area 51. However, the CIA's "unofficial" black budget has been estimated to be closer to $1.7 trillion a year, dwarfing the "official" black budget. [132] It is out of this "unofficial" black budget that the CIA funds projects housed and/or controlled out of the S-4 facility.

According to whistleblowers, the S-4 had five levels. The first level housed the nine hangars, within which were various flying saucer craft under development and testing. Members of MJ-12 had living quarters at the third level of S-4 where they could stay for extended periods to directly observe projects and make collective decisions. The fifth level was where extraterrestrials were being housed.

As mentioned earlier, the CIA had "primary responsibility for all security" at Area 51. In building two facilities, one at Groom Lake that would house aerospace projects using conventional technologies, and another more classified facility researching non-conventional or exotic technologies, the CIA had the means to deceive succeeding generations of Congressmen as to what was happening at Area 51. Any prying members of Congress wanting to follow up on rumors of UFO/extraterrestrial projects at Area 51 would be taken on a tour of the Groom Lake facility. They would be shown some of the most sensitive spyplanes such as the U-2, Oxcart and their successors, which the CIA in all seriousness would claim were national security secrets essential for the defense of the USA. The CIA would tell members of Congress that the CIA encouraged rumors of UFOs at Area 51 to distract foreign powers and the American public from learning the truth about the CIA's advanced spyplane technologies.[133] The CIA's ruse was convincing. There has never been a Congressional investigation of Area 51 to ascertain what was happening there. All of the operations had been sanctioned by President Eisenhower himself in 1954-1955.

Eisenhower understood that "black world" [in the sense of highly classified and unacknowledged] covert operations required a degree of separation from the "white world" of conventional politics. As President, Eisenhower would sometimes be in a situation where he would have to deny any U.S. official involvement in international events. This might be despite direct but covert CIA action in orchestrating such events. A good example was the CIA covert program to promote the 1956 Hungarian Revolution. This was eventually crushed by the Soviet Union with CIA agents being rounded up and executed. Eisenhower would have to officially deny any U.S. involvement in promoting such events.

As a former military man, Eisenhower knew well the importance of separating 'black' and 'white' worlds during a war. During the Cold War, his advisors recommended that this separation was vital in the unchartered waters of covert programs involving extraterrestrial life and technology. Covert teams would have to be trained and sent around the world to find and retrieve any extraterrestrial artifacts. There were some compelling reasons behind the CIA and MJ-12 being granted a remote facility to conduct covert operations. Soon after giving the CIA the authority to establish Area 51, however, Eisenhower would regret his decision to hand over responsibility of UFO/extraterrestrial related projects to MJ-12 and the CIA.

Eisenhower's Confrontation with MJ-12 over S-4

In May 2013, a retired CIA agent came forward to reveal in video testimony before six retired members of the U.S. Congress that President Eisenhower quickly grew frustrated over his lack of knowledge over what was happening at S-4.[134] The agent alleged that Eisenhower sought to gain information from the MJ-12 control group about alien-related projects at the S-4 facility. When denied the requested information, Eisenhower allegedly authorized a personal message that the agent and his immediate superior would deliver to those in charge at Area 51 and S-4. The message was a direct threat that the President would authorize a military invasion of Area 51 and S-4 if his request for information was not carried out.

The former CIA agent was 77 years old at the time of his video recording and suffering from acute kidney problems. He allegedly had only several months to live. A 15 minute segment was played out of a longer interview where he went on the public record about how he was recruited by a senior CIA operative located out of Langley, Virginia, to work with the CIA on the issue of extraterrestrial life.[135] At the time of his recruitment in 1958, he had just completed training at the U.S. Army Signal Training Center, and began working as an Army cryptologist.

His first assignment was to examine files on UFOs and extraterrestrial life submitted from USAF base at Fort Belvoir. The files were different from the Project Blue Book files studied at Wright-Patterson Air Force Base that were eventually released to the general public.

In response to questions from UFO historian Richard Dolan, the former CIA agent went on to explain how, in 1958, he and his boss – the CIA operative – were summoned by President Eisenhower to the Oval Office. The President, who was accompanied by Vice President Nixon, told the agent and his boss that he was trying to get information about extraterrestrial life and technology. The agent testified that President Eisenhower told them: "MJ-12 was supposed to find out, but they never sent reports to him." [136] President Eisenhower allegedly went on to say:

> We called the people in from MJ-12, from Area 51 and S-4, but they told us that the government had no jurisdiction over what they were doing…. I want you and your boss to fly out there. I want you to give them a personal message…. I want you to tell them, whoever is in charge, I want you to tell them that they have this coming week to get into Washington and to report to me. And if they don't, I'm going to get the First Army from Colorado. We are going to go over and take the

base over. I don't care what kind of classified material you got. We are going to rip this thing apart. [137]

In response to Dolan's question, "Eisenhower was going to invade Area 51?" the CIA agent confirmed that Eisenhower indeed planned to so with the First Army. [138]

After traveling to Area 51 and S-4, the CIA agent said that he saw several garage-type doors with flying saucers behind them. He described seeing a Gray alien at the S-4 facility that his boss "partially interviewed". Upon returning to the White House, the agent and his boss relayed what they had seen at S-4. Significantly, the FBI Director, J. Edgar Hoover, was also present during the debriefing. According to the CIA agent, Eisenhower was shocked from what he had learned.

Basically, in the three years since Eisenhower had authorized the transfer of Area 51 from the Atomic Energy Commission to the CIA, the latter had built a highly classified facility there to house UFO/extraterrestrial related projects. Various corporations such as Lockheed would be involved in the highly classified reverse engineering projects that would be conducted at S-4. While the CIA provided the funding, security and institutional support for S-4 projects, it was MJ-12 that was ultimately in charge of the projects at S-4. Yet MJ-12 was not cooperating in sharing information with the President.

Eisenhower's decision to approach the CIA for information about what was happening at S-4 is very revealing. It shows that the most secretive information concerning extraterrestrial life and technology was no longer under direct Presidential oversight, as it had been during the Truman administration. It was now being managed in a way that required the President to go through the CIA to find out what was happening. The decision to give control over security for Area 51 facilities to the CIA, rather than to one of the military services, had quickly turned into a tragic mistake by Eisenhower.

The decision, along with the reorganization of government recommended by Nelson Rockefeller, had given MJ-12 the means to create its own state within a state. Corporations, rather than scientific/military institutions, would provide expertise for the most sensitive projects out of Area 51.

The CIA agent's testimony identifies how unsatisfactory this arrangement had become for the President. It was only through confronting MJ-12 with threats of a military invasion that Eisenhower could learn what was happening at S-4. While Eisenhower had succeeded in learning what was happening in 1958 it was only a brief tactical victory. As a military man, he knew the strategic consequences of MJ-12 enjoying total autonomy at Area 51, and not reporting up the chain of command. Eisenhower's successors might not be as successful in resorting to a blunt military threat against MJ-12 and Area 51. The "black world" of covert extraterrestrial programs created by MJ-12 with CIA assistance, was now fully insulated from the "white world" of conventional American politics.

As we will see with further whistleblower testimony, from 1958 until his retirement in January 1961, Eisenhower was unable to change the situation. After the 1960 Presidential election, Eisenhower felt compelled to share his concerns in a general way with his farewell speech to the nation. It would be what he shared privately, however, with President-elect Kennedy, which would have the most dramatic effect on American history.

Endnotes Chapter 3

[83] See Wilbert Smith, "Memorandum to the Controller of Telecommunications," http://www.rexresearch.com/smith/magnet.htm

[84] Available online at: www.majesticdocuments.com/pdf/eisenhower_briefing.pdf

[85] See Stanton Friedman, *Operation Majestic-12 and the United States Government's UFO Cover-up* (Marlow and Co, 1996) 68.

[86] The Truman Memo is available online at: http://majesticdocuments.com/pdf/truman_forrestal.pdf

[87] Friedman, *Operation Majestic-12 and the United States Government's UFO Cover-up,* 65.

[88] Charles Berlitz and William Moore, *The Roswell Incident* (Grosset & Dunlap, 1980).

[89] Eisenhower Briefing Document, available online at: www.majesticdocuments.com/pdf/eisenhower_briefing.pdf

[90] Friedman, *Operation Majestic-12 and the United States Government's UFO Cover-up,* 54.

[91] Available online at: http://www.majesticdocuments.com/pdf/cutler_twining.pdf

[92] Even though the document was found in a box of official records at the National Archives, it does not have the standard control number. This has led to some claiming it was planted in the National Archives and is a hoax, but that is unlikely given NARA security procedures. See: http://www.ufoforhumanrights.com/mj-12.php . For a NARA statement on the memo, go to: http://www.archives.gov/foia/ufos.html#mj12

[93] Available online at: http://www.majesticdocuments.com/pdf/cutler_twining.pdf

[94] Smith's memo is available online at: http://www.majesticdocuments.com/pdf/smithmemo-21nov51.pdf

[95] Vannevar Bush's biography available online at: http://en.wikipedia.org/wiki/Vannevar_Bush

[96] Available online at: http://www.majesticdocuments.com/pdf/jointlogisticplan_majestic.pdf

[97] See https://en.wikipedia.org/wiki/Advisory_Committee_on_Government_Organization

[98] Seymour Hersch, *The Price of Power,* http://www.theatlantic.com/past/docs/issues/82dec/hersh.htm

[99] MJ-12 meetings at the Battelle Institute was first revealed by Michael Wolf. See: http://www.drboylan.com/wolfqut2.html

[100] Available online at:
http://www2.gwu.edu/~nsarchiv/NSAEBB/NSAEBB434/
[101] *The Central Intelligence Agency and Overhead Reconnaissance: The U-2 and Oxcart Programs, 56.* Available online at: http://tinyurl.com/q8vesmn
[102] *The Central Intelligence Agency and Overhead Reconnaissance: The U-2 and Oxcart Programs.* Available online at:
http://www2.gwu.edu/~nsarchiv/NSAEBB/NSAEBB434/
[103] *The Central Intelligence Agency and Overhead Reconnaissance: The U-2 and Oxcart Programs, 59* Available online at: http://tinyurl.com/q8vesmn
[104] Source: Defense Technical Information Center (DTIC), 'National Industrial Security Program Operating Manual Supplement.' For online reference go to:
http://www.bibliotecapleyades.net/sociopolitica/sociopol_usap.htm
April 1, 1999, Washington Times, '$3,400,000,000,000 Of Taxpayers' Money Is Missing'
[105] For more information into the Lazar story and controversy surrounding it, see: http://www.thewhyfiles.net/boblazar.htm and
http://www.classicufo.com/blog/2013/02/the-bob-lazar-conundrum-is-there-any-truth-to-lazars-claims/
[106] See: "New Element 115 Takes a Seat at the Periodic Table,"
http://science.time.com/2013/08/28/new-element-115-takes-a-seat-at-the-periodic-table/
[107] See Norio Harakaya, "My Recollections of the Enigmatic Bob Lazar,"
http://rense.com/general72/recoll.htm
[108] See Michael Salla, "Testimony of CIA assassin recruited from Navy SEALs goes online with documents," http://tinyurl.com/pob2mot
[109] See Michael Salla, "Cheney taken inside S-4 to view flying saucers & EBE bodies," http://tinyurl.com/qx8jqf3
[110] Available online in 16 parts at:
http://www.youtube.com/watch?v=holCY20CtNA
[111] Richard Boylan, "The Man Who "Outed" the U.S. Saucer Program: Colonel Steve Wilson:" http://www.drboylan.com/colbirb2.html
[112] A summary of Steve Wilson's testimony is available at:
http://www.drboylan.com/colbirb2.html
[113] See Richard Boylan, "The Man Who "Outed" the U.S. Saucer Program: Colonel Steve Wilson:" http://www.drboylan.com/colbirb2.html
[114] For an excellent summary of Burisch's claims and experiences, see Project Camelot, "Dan Burisch Summary",
http://projectcamelot.org/dan_burisch_summary.html
[115] For a list of documents featuring research and analysis of Burisch's claims, go to: http://www.bibliotecapleyades.net/esp_autor_burisch.htm . See also William Hamilton, "Project Aquarius and the Story of Dan Burisch,"
http://www.bibliotecapleyades.net/dan_burisch/esp_dan_burisch_18.htm

[116] For an article on Victor's claims go to: "Alien Interview: Video Hoax or Real Thing," http://exopolitics.org/alien-interview-video-hoax-or-real-thing/
[117] The video is available online at: http://youtu.be/a7uqP46zdsA
[118] Available online at: http://youtu.be/QdrDfSBy-2c
[119] George Hunt Williamson, *Road in the Sky* (N. Spearman, 1959) 150-51.
[120] Michael Wolf, *Catchers of Heaven* (Dorrance Pub Co, 1996) Available on Amzon.com at: http://www.amazon.com/The-Catchers-Heaven-A-Trilogy/dp/0805939075 For a review, see Neil Gould, http://exonews.org/catchers-of-heaven-dr-michael-wolf/
[121] For a detailed study of Wolf's claims, see Chris Stoner, The UFO Cover Up and ET Reality," http://www.bibliotecapleyades.net/sociopolitica/esp_sociopol_mj12_4_1.htm
[122] Stoner, The UFO Cover Up and ET Reality," http://www.bibliotecapleyades.net/sociopolitica/esp_sociopol_mj12_4_1.htm
[123] Neil Gould interviewed de la Messuziere and posted his testimony online at: http://www.youtube.com/watch?feature=player_embedded&v=yOR1NNg90c0
[124] Veteran UFO Researcher claims to have witnessed several of the phone conversations that Wolf had with Puthoff
[125] For Edgar Fouche's credentials and testimony visit: http://www.alienscientist.com/fouche.html
[126] http://www.alienscientist.com/forum/showthread.php?171-Dr.-%28-%29-Michael-Wolf-Kruvant-quot-Catchers-of-Heaven-quot-Hoaxer-Or-Not
[127] Wolf conducted an extensive number of interviews with Paola Harris who recorded them. He told her of his close relationship with James Jesus Angleton. For one of Harris' interviews with Wolf, visit: http://www.paolaharris.com/newolfint.htm
[128] Email from Maurizio Baiata, September 11, 2013.
[129] 50 United States Code 403j(b). For an online database of all federal statutes codified in the USC, go to: http://www.access.gpo.gov/uscode/index.html
[130] See Michael Salla, "The Black Budget Report," http://exopolitics.org/Report-Black-Budget.htm
[131] See "U.S. spy network's successes, failures and objectives detailed in 'black budget' summary," http://tinyurl.com/pfqdzx7
[132] See Michael Salla, "The Black Budget Report," http://exopolitics.org/Report-Black-Budget.htm
[133] See Howard Blum, *Out There: The Government's Secret Quest for Extraterrestrials* (Simon & Schuster, 1992) 264.
[134] For an article about the CIA agent's testimony, see: "Eisenhower threatened to invade Area 51 former U.S. Congress members hear testimony," http://exopolitics.org/eisenhower-threatened-to-invade-area-51-former-us-congress-members-hear-testimony/

---

[135] Video segment is available online at: http://youtu.be/GX0FaindPPo
[136] Agent's testimony available online at: http://youtu.be/GX0FaindPPo
[137] Agent's testimony available online at: http://youtu.be/GX0FaindPPo
[138] Agent's testimony available online at: http://youtu.be/GX0FaindPPo

Chapter 4

Eisenhower Warns Kennedy about MJ-12

Figure 16. President Eisenhower meets President-Elect Kennedy on Dec 6, 1960

John F. Kennedy Elected U.S. President

On November 8, 1960, Senator John F. Kennedy won the U.S. Presidential election by the closest margin in history. During the two and a half month transition period, the President-Elect would meet with outgoing President Dwight D. Eisenhower twice: on December 6, 1960 and on January 19, 1961. During both meetings, Kennedy and Eisenhower would begin private discussions without their respective staffs. They would then adjourn to the Cabinet Room, along with key officials, to discuss a variety of national security issues. In those private meetings, Eisenhower would share with Kennedy some of the most troubling political problems and challenges confronting the Presidency.

Among the issues discussed was something that the public first learned about during Eisenhower's farewell speech on January 17, 1961: the danger posed by the military-industrial complex to American civil "liberties and democratic processes."[139] Only two days after issuing his startling public warning, and only one day before Kennedy's inauguration, Eisenhower had the second of his two meetings with Kennedy. In the second meeting, Eisenhower privately explained the deeper reasons for his concern about the military-industrial complex.

Kennedy would learn directly from the former five-star general and two-term President that the military-industrial complex had taken control over an issue so highly classified that relatively few people in the vast Federal bureaucracy had the necessary security clearance to know about it. The general public, furthermore, did not even take the issue seriously. The issue concerned the UFO phenomenon, and the alleged advanced technologies that had been recovered from UFO crashes. These technologies were being secretly reverse engineered in secure military-corporate facilities. Also, some of the extraterrestrial life forms piloting these craft had been retrieved alive and were being held in secure facilities.

Most troubling to Eisenhower was that the secret committee (Majestic-12 Group), he helped set up to handle the UFO phenomenon, had basically cut him out of the loop. The Office of the President, the head of the U.S. executive branch of government, was now unable to monitor an issue whose importance was more highly classified than the Hydrogen Bomb.[140] Eisenhower would certainly have gone on to share with Kennedy some or all of the details of what happened with the creation of the S-4 facility at Area 51, and the refusal of the MJ-12 Group to share information about UFO/extraterrestrial projects there. Also he surely would have shared with Kennedy his own threat to invade Area-51 to get to the bottom of what was happening at S-4.

Eisenhower and Kennedy would have reminisced about their first meeting in the summer of 1945 when Kennedy was a guest of Secretary of the Navy, James Forrestal. Perhaps it was at, or because of, a meeting between Forrestal and Eisenhower that Kennedy first learned about the Nazi programs involving extraterrestrial technologies. Kennedy was certainly aware of Operation Paperclip and the U.S. effort to continue some of the Nazis advanced technology programs, including the design and production of flying saucer-type craft. Eisenhower may have also recalled or been reminded that Kennedy, while a freshman congressman, had been briefed about the Roswell crash back in 1947.

Kennedy was no stranger to some of the information Eisenhower would be sharing. Kennedy's friendship with James Forrestal, suggested that sensitive information had been shared. Forrestal had gone on to become a founding member of Majestic-12 while Kennedy became a Congressman. It would have been easy for Forrestal to share much of what he had learned with Kennedy. Indeed, Forrestal's eagerness to share classified information about UFOs and extraterrestrial life was likely a direct factor in his sacking as Secretary of Defense in March 1949, and his death two months later.

All the knowledge Kennedy acquired over the years about the extraterrestrial issue, would have enabled Eisenhower to get him up to speed quickly on the nature of the problem involving Majestic 12 and the S-4 facility. Eisenhower would reveal details of the threat posed by the military-industrial complex to Kennedy, something that Eisenhower could only generally describe in his upcoming farewell speech to the nation.

Eisenhower's private sessions with Kennedy set the latter on a course of action that would have him directly confront the usurpers of Presidential Executive Power. This culminated abruptly on the fateful day, November 22, 1963. How can we be certain of this? That is what documents and direct witnesses reveal about Kennedy's short but tumultuous Presidency. First, let me begin with what it was that President Eisenhower told the American public in his farewell address, and what he shared privately with Kennedy in one or both of their private meetings during the Presidential transition period.

Eisenhower's Public Warning about the Military-Industrial Complex

On January 17, 1961 President Eisenhower gave, what was perhaps the most important speech in his long and distinguished career. In it, he alerted the American public to the growing power and influence of what he called the military-industrial-complex, and the dangers it posed to the democratic processes and civil liberties of the United States.

Eisenhower described the phenomenal growth of the armaments industry and its insatiable need for ever more powerful technologies to supply the U.S. military:

> Until the latest of our world conflicts, the United States had no armaments industry. American makers of plowshares could, with time and as required, make swords as well. But now we can no longer risk emergency improvisation of national defense; we have been compelled to create a permanent armaments industry of vast proportions. Added to this, three and a half million men and women are directly engaged in the defense establishment. We annually spend on military security more than the net income of all United States corporations. [141]

Figure 17. Screenshot of Eisenhower's Farewell Address

Eisenhower then discussed the dangers posed by the military-industrial complex:

> In the councils of government, we must guard against the acquisition of unwarranted influence, whether sought or unsought, by the military-industrial complex. The potential for the disastrous rise of misplaced power exists and will persist. We must never let the weight of this combination endanger our liberties or democratic processes. We should take nothing for granted. Only an alert and knowledgeable citizenry can compel the proper meshing of the huge industrial and military machinery of defense with our peaceful methods and goals, so that security and liberty may prosper together. [142]

So far, there is nothing new here since most have long known of Eisenhower's concerns over the influence of the military-industrial complex and the dangers that it poses to American "liberties or democratic processes." Most analysts have concluded that it was a clear warning about the growing power of the armaments industry to successfully lobby the U.S. Congress for favorable policies. Indeed, Geoffrey Perret, one of Eisenhower's biographers, revealed in an earlier draft of his farewell speech, that Eisenhower had described the danger posed by the "military-industrial-congressional complex."[143] The "congressional" reference was dropped so as to not antagonize currently elected officials.

Was it the armaments industry and its power to influence the U.S. Congress that Eisenhower was specifically warning the U.S. public about, or did Eisenhower have something even more specific in mind when he revealed the dangers posed by the military-industrial complex? According to someone who served directly under Eisenhower in the White House, the answer to both questions is yes.

Stephen L. Lovekin (1940-2009) worked as a practicing attorney in North Carolina, and served in the U.S. Army Reserve as a Major in the Judge Advocate's Office.[144] Most significant was Lovekin's earlier military service as an enlisted man. He was assigned to the White House Army Signal Agency in May, 1959, as a technical specialist, and served in both the Eisenhower and Kennedy administrations until August, 1961. The task of the U.S. Army Signals Corps was to maintain open communication channels for President Eisenhower at all times.

It was the men of the White House Army Signal Agency who spent the most time with Eisenhower, the much-revered five star Army General. More importantly, Eisenhower could let down his guard with them because they were reliable, traveled with him and were well trained in handling highly classified material. Eisenhower could trust these men to maintain the confidentiality and integrity of White House communications while he was traveling, and could share in confidence secrets that even senior members of Congress were not briefed about.

In an interview with Canadian UFO researcher, Grant Cameron, Lovekin reveals what he was told by Eisenhower at Camp David:

> We would sit around with him when we were at Camp David, and he knew who each and every one of us by name. That was the great thing about being under him. I was just a Sergeant at the time. I was still privy to some stuff that some people wouldn't be privy to. [145]

One of the secrets he was privy to concerned the UFO issue.

Lovekin first received public attention when he came forward as a witness for the Disclosure Project run by Dr. Stephen Greer. In a recorded interview and later in public testimony, Lovekin revealed his own direct knowledge of President Eisenhower's strong interest in the UFO issue and concern about how it was being handled. In an interview, Steven Greer asked Lovekin whether Eisenhower "showed particular interest in this subject?" Lovekin's reply details how compartmentalized the UFO issue had become under Eisenhower:

> Very, very much interest. In fact, I would say that this subject was probably among his highest of interest at that time. Yes, indeed. Reports about these UFOs were not terribly rare…. What happened was not one particular agency could handle dealing with the entire subject matter, dealing with the engineering portion, to sighting information, to reporting it into Bluebook. The whole process of dealing with the UFO phenomenon could not be handled any more by one agency and so in order to keep it alive it was given to various parts of the

99

government to work on. And I guess that they thought that they could also keep the intelligence factor as secret as possible by giving agencies a little bit here and a little bit there. And that type of compartmentalization oftentimes is done with matters like this.[146]

Most relevant is what Lovekin had to say about how Eisenhower felt about his loss of control of the UFO issue:

But what happened was that Eisenhower got sold out. Without him knowing it he lost control of what was going on with the entire UFO situation. In his last address to the nation I think he was telling us that the Military Industrial complex would stick you in the back if you were not totally vigilant. And I think that he felt like he had not been vigilant. I think he felt like he trusted too many people. And Eisenhower was a trusting man. He was a good man. And I think that he realized that all of a sudden this matter is going into the control of corporations that could very well act to the detriment of this country.[147]

Lovekin then went on to describe Eisenhower's deep frustration over how the UFO issue had been taken from his control:

This frustration, from what I can remember, went on for months. He realized that he was losing control of the UFO subject. He realized that the phenomenon or whatever it was that we were faced with was not going to be in the best hands. As far as I can remember, that was the expression that was used, "It is not going to be in the best hands." That was a real concern. And so it has turned out to be...[148]

Lovekin's testimony is highly significant if we recall that he had begun to serve in the Eisenhower White House in May 1959. He was therefore speaking about the final period of Eisenhower's presidency. Lovekin began serving roughly a year after Eisenhower's confrontation with MJ-12 over the S-4 facility. His testimony gives us an insight into what Eisenhower felt and was thinking about after the dramatic confrontation. Lovekin reveals that Eisenhower knew that he had lost control of the UFO/extraterrestrial issue. What would he do about it?

Eisenhower's growing frustration over the loss of control of the UFO/extraterrestrial issue to MJ-12 overlapped with the campaign and election of John F. Kennedy. Based on Lovekin's testimony, we can conclude that during the Presidential transition period, Eisenhower was deeply unhappy about how the UFO issue had been taken over by MJ-12 that increasingly turned to the corporate world for contracting out the most highly classified projects involving extraterrestrial life and technology.

The office of the President had been shut out of a topic that had become deeply compartmentalized, corporatized, and out of the reach of the best minds in America. Even senior military leaders were no longer in the loop about the deepest secrets and projects controlled by MJ-12. Eisenhower had made the momentous decision to warn the American public on January 17, three days before leaving office. What would he privately say to President-elect Kennedy?

Eisenhower Privately Warns Kennedy about MJ-12

There is no public transcript of the private conversations between Kennedy and Eisenhower during the Presidential transition period. We do know that they officially met twice (December 6, 1960 and January 19, 1961) to have private meetings before adjourning to the Cabinet Room to discuss transition issues with their respective staffs. Here is what Arthur Schlesinger, Jr., a Special Assistant in the Kennedy Administration, had to say about their first meeting:

> The President-elect prepared himself with great care, and the two men talked by themselves for seventy-five minutes before walking arm-in-arm into the Cabinet Room where Clifford and Persons were waiting.[149]

In that initial 75 minute meeting, Eisenhower and Kennedy could have discussed many topics in total privacy. It would not be surprising if the informal Roswell UFO Crash briefing that Kennedy allegedly received, according to the Interplanetary Phenomenon Unit Report, came up as a matter of discussion. If the report is genuine, Eisenhower would certainly have read it given his leadership role as Army Chief of Staff at the time. If Eisenhower was disgruntled over the way the UFO/extraterrestrial issue had been subsequently handled by the MJ-12 group set up to oversee the issue, he would not have wasted any time in sharing his concerns at his first private meeting with Kennedy.

It is perhaps their second meeting which was the most significant, coming as it did two days after Eisenhower's farewell address and his military-industrial complex warning. Schlesinger writes:

> On January 19 Kennedy held a final meeting with Eisenhower. They talked alone and then met with their advisors in the Cabinet Room. The discussion concentrated on points of crisis, and especially on the mounting difficulties on points of crisis, and especially on the mounting difficulties in Laos.[150]

It is hard to believe that President Eisenhower, deeply concerned as he was about how the UFO/extraterrestrial issue was being handled, and the seriousness he attached to it, would not have privately revealed the full extent of the problem to Kennedy. It is equally difficult to believe that Kennedy would not have inquired further into what Eisenhower specifically had in mind regarding his warning about the military-industrial complex two days earlier. Was it just the armaments industry's influence over Congress that was a problem, or was there a bigger problem that Kennedy had to tackle?

If Kennedy had indeed received an informal briefing about the Roswell crash in 1947, he would have naturally inquired about what had subsequently happened. Kennedy would have known that Eisenhower had been officially briefed about the crash in his capacity as Army Chief of Staff. In either this second meeting, or perhaps both of their private meetings, UFOs and Kennedy's Roswell crash briefing would have been discussed.

Regardless of the question of whether Kennedy had been informally briefed or not about the Roswell Crash, Eisenhower would certainly have given him details on the precise nature of the threat posed by the military-industrial complex that he just warned the American public about. From Lovekin's testimony, it is clear the loss of Presidential authority over the UFO issue deeply concerned Eisenhower.

Figure 18. President Eisenhower and President-Elect Kennedy at their January 19, 1961 Meeting

It is at their second private meeting that Eisenhower most likely shared information about his 1958 confrontation with Majestic-12 over control of the S-4 facility. The fact that Eisenhower had to threaten to invade the facility with the U.S. First Army would surely have alarmed Kennedy. Consequently, part of Eisenhower's private discussions with Kennedy, especially on January 19, 1961, would almost certainly have mentioned the control group formed to take responsibility over the UFO issue – Majestic-12. Kennedy would soon face the same problem that Eisenhower had unsuccessfully grappled with since 1958. Eisenhower perhaps shared some insights and strategies for how Kennedy could tackle the problem. They would meet again after Kennedy took office. There would be more opportunities for the two Presidents to strategize over how to deal with the Majestic-12 Group.

If Kennedy had been privately warned by Eisenhower about Majestic-12, then speeches he gave or policies he enacted as President would yield clues as to Kennedy's efforts to deal with the situation. Up until recently, there has been no documentary trail to conclusively prove that Kennedy had either an interest in the UFO issue, or implemented policies to take control over this issue from an unknown control group called MJ-12 or some other name. The release of Freedom of Information Act (FOIA) documents, leaked government documents and first hand witness accounts has changed all that.

What emerges in the chapters ahead is clear evidence of multiple attempts by President Kennedy to learn about and gain control of the UFO issue. Behind these policies and speeches lies evidence that President Kennedy knew that some UFOs were extraterrestrial in origin, and the technologies involved would forever change life on this planet as we know it. President Kennedy, acting upon Eisenhower's public and private warnings, began a concerted effort to reestablish Presidential control over the UFO issue. Like Eisenhower before him, Kennedy would have his own confrontation with Majestic-12. It would not turn out as well for Kennedy as it had for Eisenhower.

Endnotes Chapter 4

---

[139] "Eisenhower's Farewell Speech", available online at:
http://mcadams.posc.mu.edu/ike.htm
[140] See Wilbert Smith Memorandum for his comments about the security classification of the UFO phenomenon. Source:
http://www.majesticdocuments.com/pdf/smithmemo-21nov51.pdf
[141] "Eisenhower's Farewell Speech", available online at:
http://mcadams.posc.mu.edu/ike.htm
[142] "Eisenhower's Farewell Speech", available online at:
http://mcadams.posc.mu.edu/ike.htm
[143] Ledbetter, James (25 January 2011). "Guest Post: 50 Years of the "Military–Industrial Complex"". *Schott's Vocab*. New York Times. Retrieved 25 January 2011.
[144] For biography of Stephen Lovekin, go to:
http://www.roswellproof.com/lovekin.html
[145] Source: http://www.presidentialufo.com/old_site/lovekin_interview.htm
[146] "Testimony of Brigadier General Stephen Lovekin," *Disclosure: Military and Government Witnesses reveal the Greatest Secrets in Modern History*, ed., Steven M. Greer (Crossing Point Inc, 2001) 234.
[147] Lovekin's testimony is available online at:
http://www.roswellproof.com/lovekin.html It is also available in Steven Greer, *Disclosure Project* (Crossing Point, 2001) 230-37.
[148] Lovekin's testimony is available online at:
http://www.roswellproof.com/lovekin.html It is also available in Steven Greer, *Disclosure Project* (Crossing Point, 2001) 230-37.
[149] Arthur Schlesinger, Jr, *A Thousand Days: John F. Kennedy in the White House* (Houghton Mifflin Co., 1965) 126.
[150] Schlesinger, Jr, *A Thousand Days,* 165.

Chapter 5

President Kennedy Challenges MJ-12 over Access to UFO Files and Projects

After President Eisenhower's dramatic farewell speech on January 17, 1961, and his final private conversation with Kennedy two days later, the new President had a good idea of the real danger to American "liberties and democratic processes." Eisenhower only alluded to the threat in his speech, but Kennedy now had the information he needed to begin the momentous challenge ahead in reining in the growing power of Majestic-12. MJ-12's power base lay hidden within the murky world of CIA covert activities and Cold War psychological operations. MJ-12's physical base of operations deep in the Nevada desert at Area 51's S-4 facility, was controlled by the CIA's covert operations and counterintelligence departments. Kennedy knew that if he was to succeed, he had to establish his authority over Cold War psychological operations, and force the CIA to cooperate with him in sharing information and access to its covert operations. Kennedy subsequently began the first phase of his strategy for regaining Presidential control over UFO and extraterrestrial related projects. Kennedy sought to bring psychological warfare operations directly under his control, and force the CIA to share classified UFO files with him.

Taking Control of Cold War Psychological Operations

Less than a month after assuming the Presidency, Kennedy showed his resolve to restructure the National Security Council, and bring all psychological warfare activities under direct Executive control. On February 19, 1961, he issued

Executive Order 10920 that abolished the Operations Coordinating Board.[151] This was a major policy decision by the young President. The Operations Coordinating Board was the primary interagency organization responsible for Cold War psychological warfare activities.[152] It was the successor to the Psychological Strategy Board that had been established by President Truman on June 20, 1951. Truman's 1951 Directive described the power of the Psychological Strategy Board:

> Directive to: The Secretary of State, The Secretary of Defense, The Director of Central Intelligence:
>
> It is the purpose of this directive to authorize and provide for the more effective planning, coordination and conduct, within the framework of approved national policies, of psychological operations.
>
> There is hereby established a Psychological Strategy Board responsible, within the purposes and terms of this directive, for the formulation and promulgation, as guidance to the departments and agencies responsible for psychological operations, of over-all national psychological objectives, policies and programs, and for the coordination and evaluation of the national psychological effort.
>
> The Board will report to the National Security Council on the Board's activities and on its evaluation of the national psychological operations, including implementation of approved objectives, policies, and programs by the departments and agencies concerned. [153]

In 1953, the name of the Psychological Strategy Board was changed to the Operations Coordinating Board. The responsibilities of the now-abolished Operations Coordinating Board were handed over to Kennedy's national security advisor, McGeorge Bundy and the Department of State.

President Kennedy's EO 10920 showed his resolve to gain control over all covert activities related to psychological warfare. Abolishing the Operations Coordinating Board showed he was willing to dismantle any government entity in order to bring its psychological warfare operations under the direct control of his national security team.

There are two documents that show the importance of psychological warfare for Majestic-12 operations. Chapter three referred to three 1952 Top Secret memos: "Joint Logistic Plan for MAJESTIC" from the Joint Chiefs of Staff. It's worth repeating that these are official government documents released through FOIA. These documents reveal that prominent among the various "plans in support of MAJESTIC" was a "psychological warfare plan."[154] While the memos do not explicitly refer to "Operation Majestic-12" as described in the Eisenhower Briefing Document and the Truman Memo, the term "Majestic" does suggest a related logistic support plan for MJ-12 by the Pentagon. Dr Robert Wood and Ryan Wood comment on the significance of these memos from the Joint Chiefs of Staff for a world-wide covert UFO retrieval plan that would have been part of Operation Majestic-12:

> Given the worldwide nature of UFOs and their priceless value if recovered, it is imperative that the J.C.S. would have a logistic plan to recover crashed saucers and pack them back to the U.S.... This report by the Joint Logistics Plans Committee, although primarily a war plan, is clearly capable of supporting crash retrieval operations for UFOs.

The three Joint Chiefs of Staff memos help confirm the close relationship between Majestic-12 operations and psychological warfare.

The second document is a leaked "Majestic" document that is yet to be officially acknowledged. The "Majestic Twelve Project: 1st Annual Report," reveals the importance that psychological cold war operations had for MJ-12 activities:

> 5. MAJESTIC SS&P are currently focused on Psy-Op development for Cold War CI activities.[155]

The "1st Annual Report" points to the importance of counter intelligence activities in Majestic-12's psychological operations plans. This provides an important insight into the activities of Majestic-12 that was firmly embedding itself into the murky world of covert operations, psychological warfare and counterintelligence. While the authenticity of the "1st Annual Report" has been contested, Kennedy's EO 10920 confirms that his administration did attempt to bring psychological Cold War operations under the control of his administration. This "1st Annual Report" gives a plausible explanation for why Kennedy may have wanted to do this. Any policies by President Kennedy to bring Cold War operations into the control of his national security team would be a direct challenge to the authority and power of MJ-12.

Kennedy Approaches the CIA Director Dulles for Information on Majestic 12

On June 28, 1961, President Kennedy wrote a Top Secret memorandum to Allen Dulles who was the Director of the CIA:

> National Security Memorandum
> To: The Director, Central Intelligence Agency

Subject: Review of MJ-12 Intelligence Operations as they relate to Cold War Psychological Warfare Plans
I would like a brief summary from you at your earliest convenience[156]

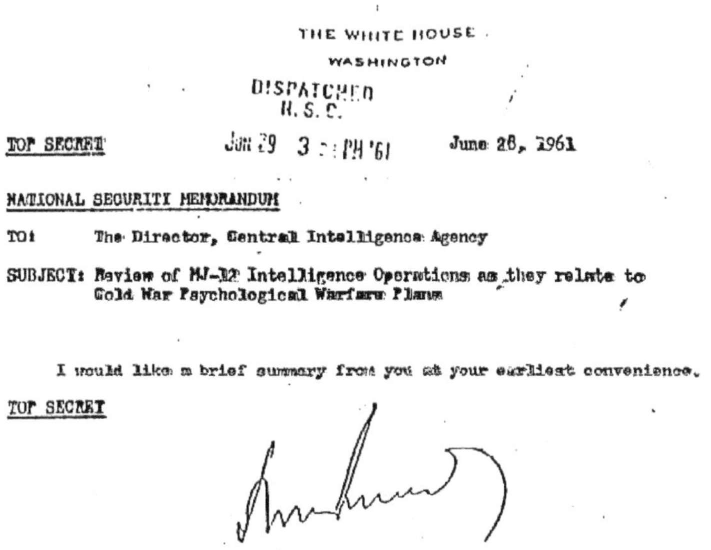

THE WHITE HOUSE
WASHINGTON
DISPATCHED
N. S. C.

TOP SECRET   Jun 29 3 : : PM '61   June 28, 1961

NATIONAL SECURITY MEMORANDUM

TO: The Director, Central Intelligence Agency

SUBJECT: Review of MJ-12 Intelligence Operations as they relate to
           Cold War Psychological Warfare Plans

      I would like a brief summary from you at your earliest convenience.

TOP SECRET

Figure 19. Kennedy's Memo to CIA Director Dulles. Source: Majestic Documents

This leaked National Security Memorandum clearly shows that in June of 1961, Kennedy wanted to learn about MJ-12 activities and the relationship with psychological warfare. While the leaked June Memorandum has not been acknowledged by the CIA (it was classified TOP SECRET), other documents from the period support its authenticity.

EO 10920 (February 1961), where Kennedy abolished the Operations Coordinating Board , helps substantiate his later June 28, 1961, National Security Memorandum concerning a review of MJ-12 activities, which he had learned involved psychological warfare. EO 10920 helps substantiate the very real concern, to be discussed later, that CIA Director Dulles believed that the future of MJ-12 was at stake due to Kennedy's initiatives.

The authenticity of the June 28, 1961 Memorandum is supported by a declassified set of three National Security Action Memorandums (NSAM) issued on the same day to the Joint Chiefs of Staff, and also forwarded to Dulles. NSAM 55-57 placed Cold War operations firmly under the control of the Joint Chiefs.[157] According to Colonel Fletcher Prouty, these memos were Kennedy's main means of gaining control over covert CIA operations. Prouty wrote:

> ... shortly after the Bay of Pigs committee had completed its hearings, the White House issued three NSAM of a most unusual and revolutionary nature. They prescribed vastly limiting stipulations upon the conduct of clandestine operations. NSAM #55 was addressed to the chairman of the JCS, and its principle theme was to instruct the chairman that the President of the United States held him responsible for all "military type" operations in peacetime as he would be responsible for them in time of war.... [T]here was no misunderstanding the full intent and weight of this document. Peacetime operations, as used in that context, were always clandestine operations.... This NSAM therefore put into the chairman's hands the authority to demand full and comprehensive briefings and an inside role during the development of any clandestine operation in which the U.S. Government might become involved.[158]

The three June 28 NSAM's support the content of the CIA Memorandum issued the same day that involved Cold War operations by MJ-12. As I will show later through a leaked and partially burned document, the three NSAMs explain why the

Joint Chiefs were excluded from the most classified UFO information by MJ-12.

As mentioned earlier, there are three 1952 Top Secret memos titled: "Joint Logistic Plan for MAJESTIC" from the Joint Chiefs of Staff. Prominent among the various "plans in support of MAJESTIC" was a "psychological warfare plan."[159] These three Joint Chiefs of Staff memos help confirm the close relationship between Majestic-12 operations and psychological warfare. Kennedy, therefore, had good reason to issue his June 28, 1961 memorandum to Dulles asking him for a review of MJ-12 psychological warfare operations.

Dulles' response to Kennedy's June 28 Memorandum was an alleged Top Secret letter issued on November 5, 1961.[160] Dulles' letter gives an overview of the MJ-12 activities with regard to psychological activities. It describes UFOs as part of "Soviet propaganda" designed "to spread distrust of the government."[161] Dulles' letter acknowledged that while it was possible some "UFO cases are of non-terrestrial origin," these did not "constitute a physical threat to national defense."[162] Most significantly, Dulles' letter said: "For reasons of security, I cannot divulge pertinent data on some of the more sensitive aspects of MJ-12 activities."[163] If genuine, Dulles' letter was giving President Kennedy only minimal information in response to his June 1961 NSAM request for a brief summary of MJ-12 activities.

RECEIVED
'JUL 2 1 2008 JFK
5-1

TOP SECRET

5 November 1961

Operations Review
by Allen W. Dulles

THE MJ-12 PROJECT

The Overview. In pursuant to the Presidential National Security Memorandum of June 28, 1961, the U.S. intelligence operations against the Soviet Union are currently active in two broad areas; aircraft launch vehicles incorporating ELINT and SIGINT capabilities; and balloon borne decoys with ECM equipment.

The Situation. The overall effectiveness about the actual Soviet response and alert status is not documented to the point where U.S. intelligence can provide a true picture of how Soviet air defenses perceive unidentified flying objects.

Informational sources have provided some detail on coded transmissions and tactical plans whose reliability is uncertain, and thus, do not give us precise knowledge of Soviet Order of Battle. Current estimates place Soviet air and rocket defenses on a maximum alert footing with air operations centered on radar and visual verification much the same as ours.

Future psychological warfare plans are in the making for more sophisticated vehicles whose characteristics come very close to phenomena collected by Air Force and NSA elements authorized for operations in this area of intelligence.

Basis for Action. Earlier studies indicated that Americans perceived U.F.O. sightings as the work of Soviet propaganda designed to convince U.S. intelligence of their technical superiority and to spread distrust of the government. CIA conducted three reviews of the situation utilizing all available information and concluded that 80% of the sighting reports investigated by the Air Force's Project Blue Book were explainable and posed no immediate threat to national security. The remaining cases have been classified for security reasons and are under review. While the possibility remains that true U.F.O. cases are of non-terrestrial origin, U.S. intelligence is of the opinion that they do not constitute a physical threat to national defense. For reasons of security, I cannot divulge pertinent data on some of the more sensitive aspects of MJ-12 activities which have been deemed properly classified under the 1954 Atomic Energy Act of 1954.

I hope this clarifies the necessity to keep current operations with CIA activities in sensitive areas from becoming official disclosure. From time to time, updates will be provided through NIE as more information becomes available.

(Signed) Allen W. Dulles

This document contains _____ pg

Copy No.   of   copies

Figure 20. DCI Dulles responds to Kennedy's June Memorandum. Source: Majestic Documents

Dulles and the Partially Burned MJ-12 Memorandum

The leaked June 28, 1961 Memorandum, EO 10920, NSAM's 55-57 and Dulles' November 1961 letter, reveal that a power struggle was occurring over Presidential Executive control of Cold War psychological warfare programs and the covert activities of MJ-12. Up until his resignation as CIA Director on November 29, 1961, Dulles was the pivotal figure in the power struggle with Kennedy over MJ-12 activities and its control of classified UFO files. This power struggle is reflected in a leaked, partially burned, draft of a memorandum allegedly rescued from a fire burning the remainder of James Angleton's files after his death on May 12, 1987. Angleton, as mentioned earlier, was the CIA chief of counterintelligence (1954-1974), and was heavily involved in providing security for the MJ-12 Group.

In late 1974, Angleton was being forced into retirement by the new CIA Director, William Colby. According to Cord Meyer in *Facing Reality*:

> December 17, Colby informs Angleton that he is relieving him of his two principal duties, his function as Chief of the Counterintelligence Staff and his responsibility for liaison with Israeli intelligence. He gives Angleton the option of remaining in the Agency in a consultant capacity or of retiring before the end of the year.... And Colby gives him two days to reconsider.[164]

On December 25, 1974, Angleton's retirement is announced to the CIA, and the news is quickly leaked to the press. Significantly, his successors soon began a process of burning Angleton's vast file collection. In 1990, Mark Riebling revealed in his book, *Wedge*, that "Angleton's successors had actually burned 99 percent of his CI files."[165] Apparently, Angleton's files were so sensitive that it was far better to simply burn them. It is not surprising that after his death, Angleton's private collection would meet the same fate as those left behind at the CIA after his retirement.

In 1989, Whitley Strieber wrote a book titled *Majestic*, about the Roswell crash and the top secret control group subsequently formed to manage UFO files. He consulted various USAF sources including his uncle, Colonel Edward Strieber, and Brigadier General Arthur Exon, who headed Wright-Patterson Air Force Base (1964-1966). Whitley Strieber learned that James Angleton was deeply involved in collecting and controlling access to UFO files. Strieber concluded he had a good idea of key events and players but could not prove it. He explains why he decided to write a fictionalized version of Roswell and subsequent events as follows:

> In the end I found myself with much more knowledge of the [Roswell] incident than I could prove. Among other things, I had formed the impression that a Central Intelligence officer, James Angleton, had been involved in an investigation of the incident in the late 1940s, but I was very far from being able to prove that, or even to suggest it in a nonfiction context.[166]

Through his independent sources, Strieber had learned that Angleton had accumulated a large collection of UFO files. In his *Majestic* book, Strieber depicted the Angleton character as the CIA's gatekeeper of UFO files. After Angleton's death in 1987, it is very plausible that the CIA believed Angleton had in his possession a collection of very sensitive UFO files that needed to be confidentially destroyed. However, a former CIA agent assigned to this highly sensitive assignment apparently did not agree.

One of Angleton's counterintelligence colleagues, who claimed to be present at the burning of Angleton's files, saved some of the collection. He sent these saved files to Timothy Cooper, a UFO researcher best known for his role in making public leaked MJ-12 documents.[167] The partially burned memorandum was sent to Cooper on June 23, 1999. In the cover letter, the agent states:

> I am a retired CIA counterintelligence officer who worked for Jim Angleton from … [text blacked out] secret files … [text blacked out] sensitive files that would connect MJ-12 to JFK's murder. This document did not exist officially and has never been disclosed within the agency. AWD [Allen Dulles] was very fearful of disclosure to unauthorized channels and leaks in the White House. I literally snatched the "Directives" from the fire and have kept them safe from review. To allow a review would compromise future directors and put the agency in a difficult position.[168]

According to Dr. Robert Wood and Ryan Wood, the burned document:

> … is an original carbon with an Eagle watermark characteristic of government work, but so far forensic laboratories have been unable to trace it…. Although no date is given, its content directly suggests the month of September. The year is estimated to be in the early 1960s and is still under investigation.[169]

The burned document dates from the Kennedy era and has the characteristics of a government document.[170] If its contents are accurate, it provides smoking gun evidence of the power struggle between Kennedy and MJ-12 over access to UFO information.

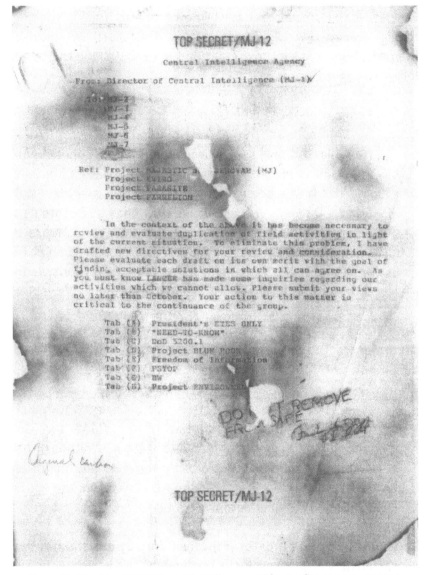

Figure 21. Top Secret CIA Memo allegedly rescued from a fire. Source: Majestic Documents

The classified Top Secret document with MJ-12 codeword access is a set of directives from the Director of the CIA who simultaneously headed the MJ-12 Special Studies Project, to six other members of the Project. These are identified on the cover page as MJ-2, MJ-3, MJ-4, MJ-5, MJ-6, and MJ-7. It says on the cover page:

> As you must know Lancer [Kennedy's Secret Service codename] has made some inquiries regarding our activities which we cannot allow. Please submit your views no later than October. Your action to this matter is critical to the continuance of the group.[171]

The document clearly acknowledges that Kennedy's efforts to gain access to UFO information soon after coming into office on January 20, 1961, actually imperiled the existence of the MJ-12 Special Studies Project/Group.

While the partially burned document has no date of issue, the authority of the writer and the political context indicates it was written shortly after Kennedy had issued his June 26, 1961 National Security Action Memorandum requesting a "Review of MJ-12 Intelligence Operations as they related to Cold War Psychological Warfare Plans."[172] The burned document acknowledged that it had "become necessary to review and evaluate duplication of field activities in light of the current situation."[173] This appears to be a reference to the June 26 NSAM review Dulles was ordered to undertake.

The burned document appeared to be a draft for a series of MJ-12 directives from Allen Dulles, who knew his time as DCI was limited due to the April, 1961, Bay of Pigs fiasco. He needed an answer from the other MJ-12 members by October, a month before he was to retire as DCI on November 29, 1961. The burned document contained a number of directives concerning how to control UFO information and ensure that it would not be shared with the "Chief Executive [President Kennedy), National Security Council Staff, department heads, the Joint Chiefs, and foreign representatives." Dulles' secret directives proscribed Kennedy's National Security team from gaining access to the most sensitive UFO files possessed by the CIA and MJ-12. Like Eisenhower before him, Kennedy's administration would be denied direct access to the S-4 facility at Area 51.

The most damning directive, drafted by Dulles and apparently approved by six other MJ-12 members is titled "Project Environment." It is a cryptic assassination directive. In full, it states:

> **Draft - Directive Regarding Project Environment - When conditions become non-conducive for growth in our environment and Washington cannot be influenced any further, the weather is lacking any precipitation ... it should be wet.**[174]

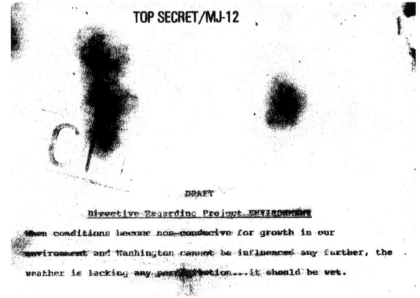

Figure 22. Draft Project Environment Directive. Source: Majestic Documents

Dr. Robert Wood who is the foremost expert in analyzing MJ-12 documents using forensic methods, has concluded that the burned document is an assassination directive. In an interview discussing the burned document, he points out that the cryptic phrase, "it should be wet" originates from Russia where the phrase "wet works" or "wet affairs" denotes someone who had been killed and is drenched with blood.[175]

The code word "wet" was later adopted by the Soviet KGB and other intelligence agencies, according to Dr. Wood. The term "it should be wet" therefore is a coded command to kill someone. In drafting this cryptic directive, Allen Dulles was seeking approval from six of his MJ-12 colleagues, to justify the assassination of any elected or appointed official in Washington D.C. whose policies were "non-conducive for growth." The directive is a pre-authorization to assassinate any U.S. President who could not "be influenced any further" to follow MJ-12 policies. The obscure language of the directive insulated the MJ-12 Group in the case of a leak. Its real intent, however, would be clear to any seasoned covert operative. A CIA veteran like James Angleton would know its real meaning and what he was being asked to do once it had been entrusted to him. No American President would be allowed again to threaten MJ-12 operations as Eisenhower did back in 1958.

While the response of other MJ-12 members to his draft is not found in leaked documents, Dulles' November 5, 1961 letter to Kennedy indicates that his secret draft of MJ-12 directives was approved. Dulles' letter firmly suggests that MJ-12 had decided not to cooperate with Kennedy. Thus, Kennedy's efforts to incorporate MJ-12 psychological warfare activities under the direct control of his National Security Advisor had been dismissed.

Kennedy's failure to pressure the CIA and MJ-12 to yield substantive information about its operations stands in stark contrast to Eisenhower's success in forcing MJ-12 to report on its activities. Eisenhower succeeded in having CIA agents travel to the S-4 facility and give him a full report back at the White House. Eisenhower, however, had to threaten to invade Area 51 with the Colorado-based U.S. First Army, a threat that MJ-12 determined was very credible. However, Kennedy's relationship with the Pentagon was very different to Eisenhower's, and there was little chance that he could likewise threaten MJ-12 with a military take-over of the S-4 facility. If Kennedy continued in his efforts to follow in Eisenhower's path and demand access to classified UFO/extraterrestrial files and projects, the draft Assassination Directive pointed to the likely consequences.

Conclusion: The CIA/MJ-12 Refusal to Cooperate with Kennedy

In summary, documents reveal that in 1961, President Kennedy attempted to gain control over intelligence activities related to Cold War psychological warfare operations. This is confirmed in Executive Order 10920, abolishing the Operations Coordinating Board that placed interagency psychological warfare plans under the control of McGeorge Bundy. It is further supported by declassified 1952 memos from the Joint Chiefs of Staff to provide logistic support for MAJESTIC psychological warfare programs,[176] and three National Security Action Memoranda issued on June 28, 1961 to place covert Cold War activities under the control of the Joint Chiefs of Staff. On the same day, June 28, Kennedy contacted Allen Dulles to request a summary of MJ-12's psychological warfare activities. Dulles' November 5 response highlighted that these activities involved the UFO issue, but declined to release sensitive information. These events are consistent with the content of the burned document which comprised eight directives restricting access to

UFO information from the President, his National Security Council Staff, including Bundy, and the Joint Chiefs of Staff. It can therefore be concluded that Allen Dulles was the official who drafted the burned document.

Sometime shortly before his November 5, 1961 letter to Kennedy, Dulles' draft set of directives had been responded to and approved by six other members of MJ-12. While Dulles and MJ-12 frustrated Kennedy's efforts to gain access to classified UFO files in late 1961, less than two years later Kennedy would embark on a new course of action that would renew his confrontation with MJ-12. This would be Kennedy's final stand against MJ-12, and it would come to a devastating climax on the fateful day of November 22. The "Assassination Directive" in the burned memo is the key to unraveling ultimate responsibility for the Kennedy assassination. Who were the six members of MJ-12 who approved Dulles' Draft Assassination Directive?

Endnotes Chapter 5

---

[151] Available online at:
http://www.presidency.ucsb.edu/ws/?pid=58858#axzz2fYI9s9Jw
[152] President Truman's Executive Order 10483 - Establishing the Operations Coordinating Board, was issued on
September 2, 1953. Available online at:
http://www.presidency.ucsb.edu/ws/index.php?pid=60573
[153] See: Harry S. Truman: "Directive Establishing the Psychological Strategy Board": http://www.presidency.ucsb.edu/ws/?pid=13808#ixzz2fYIx7UGd
[154] Available online at:
http://www.majesticdocuments.com/pdf/jointlogisticplan_majestic.pdf
[155] Available in Dr Robert Wood and Ryan Wood, *The Majestic Documents* (Wood and Wood Enterprises, 1998)
[156] Available online at:
http://www.majesticdocuments.com/pdf/kennedy_ciadirector.pdf
[157] Available online at:
http://www.jfklibrary.org/Historical+Resources/Archives/Reference+Desk/NSAMs.htm
[158] Fletcher Prouty, The Secret Team: The CIA and Its Allies in Control of the United States and the World (Skyhorse Publishing, 2008) 134-35. Also available online at: http://www.bilderberg.org/st/SecretTeamChapter04.htm
[159] Available online at:
http://www.majesticdocuments.com/pdf/jointlogisticplan_majestic.pdf
[160] "Operations Review: The MJ-12 Project," available online at:
http://www.majesticdocuments.com/pdf/mj12opsreview-dulles-61.pdf
[161] "Operations Review: The MJ-12 Project," available online at:
http://www.majesticdocuments.com/pdf/mj12opsreview-dulles-61.pdf
[162] "Operations Review: The MJ-12 Project," available online at:
http://www.majesticdocuments.com/pdf/mj12opsreview-dulles-61.pdf
[163] "Operations Review: The MJ-12 Project," available online at:
http://www.majesticdocuments.com/pdf/mj12opsreview-dulles-61.pdf
[164] Cord Meyer, *Facing Reality: From World Federalism to the CIA* (Harper and Row, 1980) 205-08
[165] Mark Riebling, Wedge: *The Secret War between the FBI and the CIA* (Alfred Knopf, 1994) 327.
[166] Whitley Strieber, *Majestic* (Tor Books, Reprint Edition, 2011) Kindle Edition.
[167] Available online at:
http://www.majesticdocuments.com/pdf/burnedmemocoverletter.pdf

[168] Letter addressed to Timothy Cooper, June 23, 1999. Available online at: http://majesticdocuments.com/pdf/burnedmemocoverletter.pdf
[169] See prefatory comments for burned memo at: http://www.majesticdocuments.com/documents/1960-1969.php
[170] The burned memorandum is available online at: http://majesticdocuments.com/documents/1960-1969.php#burnedmemo
[171] See page one of burned memorandum available at: http://www.majesticdocuments.com/pdf/burnedmemo-s1-pgs1-2.pdf
[172] "John F. Kennedy to Director, CIA," http://www.majesticdocuments.com/pdf/kennedy_ciadirector.pdf
[173] See page one of burned memorandum available at: http://www.majesticdocuments.com/pdf/burnedmemo-s1-pgs1-2.pdf
[174] Cited online at: http://www.majesticdocuments.com/pdf/burnedmemo-s1-pgs3-9.pdf
[175] Available online at: http://www.scribd.com/doc/6404101/JFK-MJ12
[176] See chapter two.

Chapter 6

Who Were Majestic-12 Members During the Kennedy Administration?

Based on the composition of Majestic-12 as outlined in the Eisenhower Briefing Document, we can develop a good idea of the likely composition of MJ-12 during the Kennedy administration. Even more importantly, we can get an answer to the question of who were the additional six members of MJ-12 that were on the distribution list of Dulles' draft directives which included the cryptic "Assassination Directive" called "Project Environment." Essentially, it was a license to kill by whomever was assigned responsibility for its implementation. In addition to Dulles, who was described as MJ-1, the other six members were described as MJ-2, MJ-3, MJ-4, MJ-5, MJ-6, and MJ-7.

In his cover letter to the six other members of MJ-12, Dulles wrote:

I have drafted some directives for your review and consideration. Please evaluate each draft on its own merit with the goal of finding acceptable solutions in which all can agree on.[177]

In the context of the above it has become necessary to review and evaluate duplication of field activities in light of the current situation. To eliminate this problem, I have drafted new directives for your review and consideration. Please evaluate each draft on its own merit with the goal of finding acceptable solutions in which all can agree on. As you must know LANCER has made some inquiries regarding our activities which we cannot allow. Please submit your views no later than October. Your action to this matter is critical to the continuance of the group.

Figure 23. Cover Letter to Burned Directives Memorandum. Source: Majestic Documents

Dulles' statement emphasizes the importance of finding solutions that "all can agree on." This indicates that the six members of the MJ-12 Group most likely consensually approved some or all of Dulles' draft directives as a collective decision.

The Eisenhower Briefing document identified 12 members of the Majestic 12 Group. These were fairly evenly distributed across three groups of individuals with different skills and backgrounds. The first group occupied important positions in the National Security Council system that had been established by President Truman in 1947. The second group included scientists and engineers who were leaders in their respective scientific disciplines. The final group was senior military officials from the three main U.S. military services: Navy, Air Force and Army. Each service had two members after the addition of General Smith to MJ-12 in October, 1950. The 12 names were listed below each other in order. This likely indicated a hierarchy of positions based on designations such as MJ-1, MJ-2, etc.

We know from the draft memo that the distribution went sequentially through the various MJ-12 positions starting with Dulles as MJ-1, up to MJ-7. The Eisenhower briefing documents have the three sub-groups of national security officials, scientists, and military officers mixed throughout the ordering. Consequently, we can expect that in addition to Dulles, the additional six members of the MJ-12 Group were a mixture of national security officials, scientists, and military officers.

One question that needs to be asked is why Dulles' draft directives were distributed to only six other members of the MJ-12 Group, rather than the full committee? One possible reason is that this list comprised the most senior members, a kind of executive committee within MJ-12. This would facilitate quick policy-making decisions if needed. Dulles' draft possesses a tone of urgency. He needed a response by October, a month before his retirement as CIA Director. So his directives needed to be fast-tracked through the MJ-12 decision-making process.

If the executive committee of MJ-12 reached a consensus on any issue, that would constitute a simple majority of seven, removing the need for additional votes from the remaining five members. Passage of the Dulles Assassination Directive could therefore have passed as a decision of MJ-12 even if not all MJ-12 members were involved in its drafting or passage. Alternatively, though less likely, given the time constraint of Dulles' impending retirement, the draft may have been forwarded to the full MJ-12 committee with a recommendation by the executive committee for a final vote.

No matter how the decision was finally made, we do know that the Dulles list of directives was passed in some form. One of the directives was mentioned in a handwritten note added to a Top Secret Memorandum issued by President Kennedy to CIA Director, John McCone on November 12, 1963.[178] The handwriting was by William Colby, the CIA Chief for Far East Asia at the time. Colby wrote: "Angleton has MJ directive." The handwriting is dated November 19, 1963 – three days before Kennedy's Assassination. The content and date strongly suggest that one of the directives, very likely the cryptic assassination directive, "Project Environment", was being used to respond to President Kennedy's latest request to the CIA. Kennedy's 1963 Memorandum to the CIA Director and its implications will be discussed in chapter nine.

Now we can ask the question, who were the men that consensually approved, in full or in part, Dulles' draft directives in late 1961? Based on scientific expertise, military position or national security appointment, we can get a solid idea of who the most likely individuals were that occupied the various MJ rankings identified in the Eisenhower Briefing Document and the burned Draft Directives Memorandum. I will identify each of the individuals that most likely occupied the different MJ-12 positions in late 1961, followed by an explanation of why they occupied these positions and their likely predecessors.

MJ-1: Allen Dulles

The first name on the Majestic-12 list identified by the Eisenhower Briefing Document was Admiral Roscoe Hillenkoetter who was Director of the CIA from 1947 to 1951. At the time of the November 1952 briefing, Hillenkoetter held the rank of Rear Admiral and was the Commander of the Third Naval District, New York. He was identified in the Briefing document as MJ-1, and was the briefing officer for President Eisenhower. It's significant that even though Hillenkoetter had been replaced by Walter Bedell Smith who was CIA director from 1950 to 1953, that Hillenkoetter remained as "MJ-1." This suggests that the MJ-12 Group operated on the principle of seniority for members who remain active in their respective careers; and that the leader of the Intelligence Community (the CIA Director at the time) could rise to the position of MJ-1.

Hillenkoetter officially retired from active military service in 1957, and very likely ceased to serve on MJ-12. His position as MJ-1 was officially taken over by Allen Dulles who was the CIA Director (1953-1961) at the time of Hillenkoetter's retirement. Dulles' position as MJ-1 was revealed in the Burned Memo.

After the drafting and passage of the Burned Memo, Dulles' position as CIA Director was taken over by John McCone in November 29, 1961. It is very likely that McCone took over the position of MJ-1 at a later date. McCone was not involved in the drafting or approval of Dulles' "Project Environment." The question of his role in its implementation is an interesting one. Once passed and assigned to James Angleton for possible implementation, MJ-12 may have simply regarded the issue as settled, and not subject to further revision.

MJ-2: Dr. Edward Teller

The second member of Majestic 12 was identified by the Eisenhower Briefing Document as Dr. Vannevar Bush. Bush was the leading scientific coordinator of the World War II era, and headed the Office of Scientific Research and Development from 1941 to 1947. He was the scientist that initiated the Manhattan Project and recruited Robert Oppenheimer to play a leading scientific role in developing the atomic bomb.[179] His second position (MJ-2) on the list suggested that a leading scientific coordinator was the second highest ranking official of MJ-12. Bush was known for his compartmentalization of classified projects. According to Friedman:

> Contrary to the normally wide-ranging access permitted in most research settings, Bush insisted that working scientists be permitted access only to the classified information they needed to do their well-defined jobs. Scientific curiosity was not sufficient reason for access to classified data beyond one's own field.[180]

At the time of the Eisenhower Briefing Document, Bush's influence was waning. President Truman decided to support the development of the Hydrogen Bomb, and the first Hydrogen Bomb device was tested on November 1, 1952, only days before Eisenhower's Presidential victory. Bush supported his friend, Robert Oppenheimer, who strongly opposed Hydrogen bomb development. Oppenheimer eventually lost his security clearance despite Bush's support. This revealed that Bush's role in the MJ-12 was coming to an end.

Bush's position as the scientific coordinator on the MJ-12 committee was very likely taken over by Dr. Edward Teller relatively soon after the Hydrogen Bomb program went ahead. Consequently, the number two position (MJ-2) during the

131

Kennedy administration was likely held by Teller. Decades later, Teller played a key role in recruiting Robert Lazar and Dan Burisch to work at the S-4 facility. This suggested that Teller retained his membership on the MJ-12 Group. In the position of MJ-12's lead scientist (MJ-2), Teller may have been among the six MJ-12 co-signers of Dulles' cryptic assassination directive.

MJ-3: Lt. General Marshall Carter

The third position on the list (MJ-3) was held by the first Secretary of Defense, James Forrestal. This suggests that MJ-3 represents the interests of the combined military services. Forrestal allegedly suffered a mental breakdown, and in March 1949 was sacked by President Truman. The official explanation of Forrestal's sacking, however, was contrived to hide serious policy disputes he held with Truman and the majority of MJ-12 members. The Eisenhower Briefing Document mentions what happened after Forrestal's 1949 death:

> The death of Secretary Forrestal on 22 May, 1949 created a vacancy which remained unfilled until 01 August, 1950, upon which date Gen Walter B. Smith was designated as permanent replacement.[181]

Curiously, Forrestal's position remained vacant for over 14 months until a "permanent replacement" could be found. No reason was given for the long delay and the choice not to appoint his successor as Secretary of Defense, Louis A. Johnson (1949–1950). Presumably, the MJ-12 committee was divided on a successor for Forrestal. President Truman had decided in May 1950 that he wanted Smith to fill the position of Director of Central Intelligence, but the onset of the Korean War in June delayed his appointment. In August, Smith was approved as the newest member of MJ-12. On October 7, Smith was sworn in as the new Director of the CIA. After leaving the CIA on February 9, 1953, Smith served as Under Secretary of State (1953-1954) and various other positions in the Eisenhower administration until his death in August, 1961.

Smith's replacement on the MJ-12 Group needed to be a senior Army officer who was briefed on the UFO/ET issue. This would maintain the balance between different military services in MJ-12. The most likely candidate was Lt. General Marshall Carter. Carter was an aide to General George Marshall when the latter was Chief of Staff of the U.S. Army during the Second World War. It was Marshall who established the Interplanetary Corps to study the extraterrestrial phenomenon in 1942 according to leaked memos discussed in chapter two. This made it very likely that Carter was briefed about alien life and technology early in his military career. Carter served as Deputy Director of the CIA from April 3, 1962 to 1965. Since the CIA was the lead government agency in managing the UFO/extraterrestrial issue, this most likely meant that Carter was again briefed on the issue. In 1965, he was promoted to Director of the National Security Agency. It is likely that Carter was recruited to the MJ-12 Group sometime between Smith's death in August, 1961 and his appointment as CIA Deputy Director in April, 1962. It is therefore possible that Carter may have been among the group of six MJ-12 members that approved "Project Environment."

MJ-4: General Curtis LeMay

The fourth name on the MJ-12 Group list (MJ-4) was General Nathan Twining. Twining was the chief of the Air Material Command (AMC) at Wright Air Field (renamed Wright-Patterson Air Force Base) at the time of the Roswell Crash. Artifacts and bodies from the crash were taken to Wright field for further study since AMC was the Army Air Force's premier facility for studying aeronautical technologies. Twining was promoted to Air Force Chief of Staff (1953-1957) and finally to Chairman of the Joint Chiefs of Staff (1957-1960).

Twining's most likely successor was General Curtis LeMay who also rose to the position of Chief of Staff to the U.S. Air Force (1961-1965). It was General LeMay who denied Senator Barry Goldwater access to Hangar/Building 18 at Wright-Patterson AFB that allegedly stored some of the Roswell Crash wreckage as well as other alien artifacts. Goldwater claimed on several occasions that it was the only time his friend, LeMay, got angry at him. Goldwater revealed that LeMay told him, "very emphatically that nobody could go in those rooms, not even he."[182] The Goldwater incident indicates that LeMay was briefed about alien life and technologies, and was the most likely Air Force officer to succeed Twining as a member of MJ-12. Critically, LeMay was on MJ-12 during the Kennedy administration, and may have been among the group of six that approved Dulles' cryptic assassination directive.

MJ-5: Lt. General Gordon Blake

The fifth name on the MJ-12 Group list (MJ-5) was General Hoyt Vandenberg who was appointed Deputy Commander in Chief of the Air Staff on June 15, 1947. This was the critical position he held during the time of the Roswell Crash, and made him a key player in the subsequent cover up. At the July 8 Press Conference where General Roger Ramey claimed the Roswell debris was a misidentified weather balloon, Ramey was clutching a telegram to Vandenberg about the cover up.[183] With the formation of the U.S. Air Force, Vandenberg became Vice Chief of Staff on October 1, 1947. He became Chief of Staff from 1948 to 1953. He died on April 2, 1954, thereby creating a new position to be filled on the MJ-12 Group. To maintain the balance between the military services, a senior Air Force officer needed to fill the vacancy – one that was already deeply familiar with the UFO/extraterrestrial issue.

A likely replacement was General Gordon Blake who at the time of Vandenberg's death was Director of Communications for the Air Force's system of global communications and navigation.[184] Blake had earlier filled key positions at Wright-Patterson AFB where he was in charge of 12 development laboratories (1951-1952), and Vice Commander of the base (1952-1953). As mentioned earlier, Wright-Patterson was the leading Air Force base for studying the Roswell wreckage and alien artifacts. While in charge of the 12 development laboratories, it is highly likely that he was involved with classified studies of the Roswell wreckage and met with MJ-12 members. Prior to the construction of the S-4 facility at Area 51 in 1955, MJ-12 used Wright-Patterson as their major base of operations. With his appointment as Director of the National Security Agency (1962-1965), Blake was promoted to Lt. General. The role of the NSA in monitoring global electronic communications made it a key agency in gaining intelligence about extraterrestrial life and technology. Blake was likely appointed as Vandenberg's replacement to MJ-12 during the Eisenhower administration. Blake may have been among the group of six that approved "Project Environment".

MJ-6: Dr. Detlev Bronk

The sixth name on the MJ-12 Group list (MJ-6) was Dr. Detlev Bronk. Bronk had established biophysics as a new scientific discipline. Among his positions was President of Johns Hopkins University (1949-1953), and President of the National Academy of Sciences (1950-1962). Bronk served on many other scientific committees. According to Friedman:

> Everywhere one looked around the Washington scientific scene in the 1950s and 1960s, there was Detlev Bronk....His primary field was aviation biology.... There was nobody better equipped at that time to deal with the question of what was special about alien bodies.[185]

Bronk was in the scientific sub-group of MJ-12. If Bronk held the position of MJ-6, as the Eisenhower Briefing document implies, then he was likely a member of the Executive Committee of MJ-12. It is therefore possible that Bronk was among the group of six that approved Dulles' cryptic assassination directive.

MJ-7: Dr. Jerome Hunsaker

The seventh name on the MJ-12 Group list (MJ-7) was Dr. Jerome Hunsaker. He was the first to design a wind tunnel and modern airship. Hunsaker was head of the Department of Aeronautics at Massachusetts Institute of Technology (1939-1951). Hunsaker, according to Friedman, "was at the very apex of the field of high-performance aircraft design, and trained many of the top names in that area."[186] Like Bronk, Hunsaker was in the scientific sub-group of MJ-12. If Hunsaker held the position of MJ-7, as the Eisenhower Briefing document implies, then he was also likely a member of the Executive Committee of MJ-12. It is possible that Hunsaker was among the group of six that approved the Project Environment directive.

Interestingly, the Eisenhower Briefing Document only emerged three months after Hunsaker's death. This suggests that one of the secret conditions for the release of the Majestic documents was the deaths of all founding members of MJ-12.

MJ-8: Vice Admiral Laurence Frost

The eighth name on the MJ-12 Group list (MJ-8) was Rear Admiral Sidney Souers. He was a close advisor to President Truman and served as the first Executive Director of the National Security Council from 1947 to 1950. He was then appointed Special Consultant to President from 1950 to 1953, and retired from government service at the end of the Truman Administration. Souers' position on MJ-12 therefore became available early in the Eisenhower administration. As a Navy Admiral, his replacement would have been a senior Navy officer briefed into the UFO/extraterrestrial issue in order to maintain the balance between different military services.

The most likely candidate to replace Souers was Rear Admiral Laurence Frost who began serving in Naval Intelligence after the Second World War 1945, and rose to become Director of Naval Intelligence (1956-1960). Frost went on to become Director of the National Security Agency (1960-1962), and was promoted to Vice-Admiral. With his senior positions in Naval Intelligence and later the NSA, Frost would have been the ideal Navy candidate to replace Souers at the start of the Eisenhower administration. Frost's likely service in the MJ-12 Group (as MJ-8) occurred during the period when Allen Dulles circulated the burned Assassination Directive for approval. If Frost held the position of MJ-8, as the Eisenhower Briefing document implies, then he was likely not a member of the Executive Committee of MJ-12. Frost was not likely among the group of six that approved Dulles' assassination directive.

MJ-9: Gordon Gray

The ninth name on the MJ-12 Group list (MJ-9) was Gordon Gray, the first Director of the Psychological Strategy Board from 1951 to 1952. As described earlier, the Operations Coordinating Board, the successor to the Psychological Strategy

Board, was abolished by Kennedy early in his administration. Gray was now Chairman of the NSC 5412 Committee, a very powerful group that approved covert Cold War operations. He became Eisenhower's National Security Advisor (1958-1961). He then served on the Foreign Intelligence Advisory Board (1961-1976). His continued government service meant that Gray almost certainly continued to serve as a member of the MJ-12 Group. If Gray held the position of MJ-9, as the Eisenhower Briefing document implies, then he was likely not a member of the Executive Committee of MJ-12. Gray may not have played a direct role in the approval of Project Environment.

MJ-10: Dr. Donald Menzel

The tenth name on the MJ-12 Group list (MJ-10) was Dr. Donald Menzel. He was a pioneer in the field of astrophysics and held various academic appointments at Harvard University (1932-1971). Friedman devoted a chapter of his book describing the surprising discovery that Menzel was a member of MJ-12. Friedman discovered evidence that Menzel had indeed led a double life as a Harvard academic and an influential government consultant on various classified projects.[187] Menzel was in the scientific sub-group of MJ-12, and did not occupy a leadership position. If Menzel held the position of MJ-9, as the Eisenhower Briefing document implies, then he was likely not a member of the Executive Committee of MJ-12. Menzel was likely not among the group of six that approved Dulles' cryptic assassination directive.

MJ-11: Lt. General John Samford

The eleventh name on the list was Lt. General Robert Montague who held the critical position of Commander of Sandia Missile Base (1947-1951) soon after the Roswell Crash.

Sandia was where some of the German scientists were based who examined UFO wreckage taken there according to the Eisenhower Briefing Document.[188] From 1946-1971, Sandia was the principal Department of Defense facility for the research, development, and testing for nuclear weapons. UFO researchers have shown that UFOs have regularly monitored and interfered with nuclear weapons facilities.[189] Roswell Army Air Field was itself the only operational nuclear bombing facility in 1947. It was logical that the Commander of Sandia would be briefed and play a significant role in the UFO/extraterrestrial issue. Montague went on to head command positions in European Command (1951-1952), Army Field Forces (1952-1955), and I Corps (1955-1957). His retirement and death in February 1958 created a vacant position in the MJ-12 Group. A senior Army officer who was familiar with the UFO/extraterrestrial issue would have likely been required to fill Montague's position to maintain the balance between different military services on MJ-12.

The most likely candidate would have been Lt. General John Samford. Samford was the Director of the National Security Agency from 1956-1960. Samford's signature appears on the cover page of the document reclassifying the Interplanetary Phenomenon Unit Report as NSA Director. Samford retired from active military service on November 20, 1960. If he did fill Montague's position, then by the time of his retirement two years later, Samford would have only been on MJ-12 for two years, which makes it possible that he would have continued on for a minimum time period until a replacement was found. If Samford held the position of MJ-11, as the Eisenhower Briefing document implies, then he was likely not a member of the Executive Committee of MJ-12. Either through retirement or ranking, Samford was not likely to have been among the group of six that approved "Project Environment."

MJ-12: Dr. Lloyd Berkner

The last name on the MJ-12 Group list (MJ-12) was Dr Lloyd Berkner. Berkner was a prominent geophysicist that developed a measuring device that has become standard in ionospheric monitoring stations. He first proposed the establishment of an International Geophysical Year in 1950 as a means for global cooperation in studying the Earth. He was President of the International Council of Scientific Unions (1957-1959) that conducted the International Geophysical Year in 1957-1958. Berkner became the first full-time President of a consortium of universities called the Associated Universities Inc., that ran the Brookhaven National Laboratory (1951-1960). Berkner was in the scientific sub-group of MJ-12, and did not occupy a leadership position. If Berkner held the position of MJ-12, as the Eisenhower Briefing document implies, then he was likely not a member of the Executive Committee of MJ-12. Berkner was likely not among the group of six that approved Dulles' assassination directive.

Majestic 12 in Different Presidential Administrations

In conclusion, at the time of the draft assassination directive by Allen Dulles concerning termination of federal officials who threatened MJ-12 Group operations, we can develop a list of the most likely members of MJ-12 and their hierarchical rank. From this list, we can deduce the most likely signatories of Dulles directive that used the cryptic title: "Project Environment." The following table summarizes the probable composition of MJ-12 over three Presidential administrations, their ranks, and the members that most likely approved Project Environment. The table is followed by a graphic showing the names and titles of the most likely group of officials and scientists on the MJ-12 Group for the first year of the Kennedy administration.

Rank	Original MJ-12 Group Members during Truman Administration (1947-1952)	Likely MJ-12 Group Members during Eisenhower Administration (1953-1960)	Likely MJ-12 Group Members during Kennedy Administration (1961-)	Signatories of Dulles' Draft Directive (1961)
MJ-1	MJ-1 Roscoe Hillenkoetter	Roscoe Hillenkoetter / Allen Dulles	Allen Dulles	Drafted the directive
MJ-2	Vannevar Bush /Edward Teller	Edward Teller	Edward Teller	Likely
MJ-3	James Forrestal/Gen Walter B. Smith	Walter B.Smith/ Marshall Carter	Marshall Carter	Likely
MJ-4	Nathan Twining	Nathan Twining	Curtis LeMay	Likely
MJ-5	Hoyt Vandenberg	Hoyt Vandenberg / Gordon Blake	Gordon Blake	Likely
MJ-6	Detlev Bronk	Detlev Bronk	Detlev Bronk	Likely
MJ-7	Jerome Hunsaker	Jerome Hunsaker	Jerome Hunsaker	Likely
MJ-8	Sidney Souers	Sidney Souers / Laurence Frost	Laurence Frost	Unlikely
MJ-9	Gordon Gray	Gordon Gray	Gordon Gray	Unlikely
MJ-10	Donald Menzel	Donald Menzel	Donald Menzel	Unlikely
MJ-11	Robert Montague	Robert Montague / John Samford	John Samford	Unlikely
MJ-12	Lloyd Berkner	Lloyd Berkner	Lloyd Berkner	Unlikely

Figure 24. Table of Likely MJ-12 Members during different Presidential administrations and drafting of Assassination Directive

Likely Majestic-12 Group (1958-61)

MJ-1. Allen Dulles MJ-2. Dr. Edward Teller MJ-3. Gen. Marshall Carter

MJ-4. Gen. Curtis LeMay MJ-5. Gen. Gordon Blake MJ-6. Dr. Detlev Bronk

MJ-7. Dr. Jerome Hunsaker MJ-8. Adm. Laurence Frost MJ-9. Gordon Gray

MJ-10. Dr. Donald Menzel MJ-11. Gen. John Samford MJ-12. Dr Lloyd Berkner

Figure 25. MJ-12 Group During first year of Kennedy Adminsitration

Endnotes Chapter 6

---

[177] See page one of burned memorandum available at:
http://www.majesticdocuments.com/pdf/burnedmemo-s1-pgs1-2.pdf
[178] The Memorandum has handwriting by William Colby stating: "Angleton has MJ directive." See: http://majesticdocuments.com/pdf/kennedy_cia.pdf .
[179] See: http://en.wikipedia.org/wiki/Vannevar_Bush#Manhattan_Project
[180] Stanton Friedman, *Top Secret/MAJIC: Operation Majestic-12 and the United States Government's UFO Cover up* (Marlowe & Co., 1996) 47.
[181] Eisenhower Briefing Document, 2. Available online at:
http://majesticdocuments.com/pdf/eisenhower_briefing.pdf
[182] Source: http://ufogrid.com/ufo/articles/barry-goldwater-ufo-files-posted
[183] Source: http://www.roswellproof.com/vandenberg.html
[184] See Wikipedia entry, http://en.wikipedia.org/wiki/Gordon_Blake
[185] Stanton Friedman, *Top Secret/MAJIC*, 48.
[186] Stanton Friedman, *Top Secret/MAJIC*, 49.
[187] Stanton Friedman, *Top Secret/MAJIC*, 26-40.
[188] Available at: http://majesticdocuments.com/pdf/eisenhower_briefing.pdf
[189] Robert Hastings, *UFOs and Nukes: Extraordinary Encounters at Nuclear Weapons Sites* (Author House, 2008).

Chapter 7

Kennedy Does an End Run around the CIA to Learn about UFOs

Introduction

Chapter 1 revealed the relationship Kennedy had with James Forrestal who, during a 1945 trip to post-war Germany, very likely introduced Kennedy to the topic of extraterrestrial life and technology. In Chapter 2, documentary evidence was introduced that President Kennedy received an informal briefing in 1947, while serving in Congress, about the Roswell UFO crash. When he was elected President in November 1960, he had at least two private meetings with President Eisenhower, including one two days after Eisenhower's January 17, 1961 farewell address. Chapter 4 gave reasons why Eisenhower would confide important information about UFOs and extraterrestrial life to Kennedy, and the dangers posed by MJ-12.

Chapter 5 showed that President Kennedy was denied access by the CIA to information about UFOs and the MJ-12 Group set up to control such information. Kennedy's June 1961 National Security Memorandum to CIA Director Dulles had not yielded any substantive information. Unknown to Kennedy, his Memorandum alerted the Majestic 12 Group to the danger posed to its operations by Kennedy's inquiries. Unlike President Eisenhower, who could use a threat to invade MJ-12's S-4 facility at Area-51 with the U.S. Army to gain information, Kennedy had to find different sources to learn about what was happening.

As Commander-in-Chief, he could gain access to any military facility around the country. Unfortunately, Area-51 was not a military facility, but a CIA facility with its own security protocols. This meant that any senior official, including the President himself, could not simply show up and demand access. Area 51 and its two facilities at Groom Lake and Papoose Lake (S-4) were part of the "black world" of covert projects. This meant that officials in the "white world" of conventional politics were denied access to maintain plausible deniability. That way, if any covert operation was exposed or ran afoul, the President could plausibly deny knowledge and responsibility. This was a problem President Kennedy would encounter if he tried accessing such facilities or requested briefings from military personnel who might have access to UFO information.

If leaked documents and whistleblower testimonies are correct, President Kennedy traveled to remote military locations to view retrieved extraterrestrial vehicles and bodies. He also apparently received messages from and even met with human-looking extraterrestrials, and arranged for his brother Robert to receive multiple briefings about UFOs and extraterrestrial life. Using his power as President and Commander-in-Chief, Kennedy was attempting an end-run around the obstacles put before him by the CIA and MJ-12 over the UFO issue.

Robert Kennedy Secretly Briefed about Extraterrestrial Life

President Kennedy relied on his brother and Attorney General, Robert Kennedy, to assist him in learning about UFOs and extraterrestrial life. It has long been known that Robert Kennedy had an interest in UFOs and personally wrote letters to constituents about them. None of Robert Kennedy's correspondence reveals that he had a personal belief that UFOs were interplanetary in origin, or that he had inside knowledge about them. Commenting on various letters written by Robert Kennedy on the UFO subject, Grant Cameron writes:

These letters, recovered mostly from the Kennedy Outer Space files, do indeed show an interest by Robert

Kennedy in the UFO story as it was being portrayed in the media in the mid 1960s. [E.g, Kennedy wrote] "I am keeping myself abreast of information developed on this subject." Without exception, however, the Kennedy letters show a man who has concluded there is no cover-up and UFOs are not extraterrestrial.[190]

This perception changed in 1997 when it first emerged that Robert had in fact received multiple secret briefings about classified UFO files and extraterrestrial life. Robert was receiving this information from a serving military officer with knowledge about UFOs and extraterrestrial life, and passing the information on to the President.

Lt. Colonel Philip Corso served as head of the U.S. Army's Foreign Technology Desk from 1961-1963. In 1997, he authored a popular book, *The Day After Roswell*, about his involvement in an officially sanctioned Army program to seed extraterrestrial technologies into the private sector.[191] From 1953 to 1957, Corso served on a number of National Security Council committees during the Eisenhower administration as the Army Liaison reporting directly to Lt. General Arthur Trudeau who was head of U.S. Army Intelligence (G-2). Interviewed shortly before his death in 1998, Corso revealed for the first time that Bobby Kennedy contacted him because of his knowledge of highly classified national security information. Corso claimed that he personally briefed Robert Kennedy on several occasions about a crashed UFO that was extraterrestrial in origin, and whose technology was secretly being reverse engineered. In his interview recorded on video, Corso said:

> I discussed this very thoroughly with Bobby Kennedy, the Attorney General, the President's brother... He knew about the flying saucers, I talked to him about it. I used

147

to meet him when he was Attorney General right in his office... What went to Bobby went to the President also.

Corso was aware that Robert Kennedy was a direct conduit to the President who was being briefed by his brother about what Corso was revealing.

Corso further explained in the interview that the meeting(s) happened in 1962, soon after Corso had testified on a Senate Committee about classified national security issues. At the time, Corso was in charge of the Foreign Technology Desk, and reported directly to General Trudeau who then headed the Army's Research and Development Division. Corso explained that he agreed to testify on the condition that his testimony was to be relayed directly to the Kennedy brothers.

According to Corso, he was contacted soon after by Robert Kennedy who wanted to learn more about Corso's knowledge and activities. Robert Kennedy's role in learning about UFOs made him a key figure in informing President Kennedy about extraterrestrial life and technology.

What is not well known is that Corso had previously served as General Trudeau's military liaison to the Psychological Strategy Board, and its successor, the Operations Coordinating Board. Both of these organizations specialized in Psychological Warfare operations and were integral to MJ-12's covert programs involving extraterrestrial life and technology. As a former intelligence officer working directly under the head of the Army's Head of Intelligence, Lt. General Arthur Trudeau, Corso was very familiar with covert operations and psychological warfare, and how these applied to UFOs and extraterrestrial life. Corso was likely briefing Robert Kennedy on all these aspects of CIA and MJ-12 operations. The information that was being passed to President Kennedy by his brother from Corso, would yield important insights into how the UFO/extraterrestrial issue was being handled by the CIA and MJ-12 Group.

Whistleblower Reports that President Kennedy Saw UFO Crash Wreckage and Alien Artifacts

The claim that Kennedy had knowledge of UFO crash retrieval operations and extraterrestrial life is supported by additional whistleblower testimony. In his book *Need to Know*, Timothy Good cites a reliable military source that Kennedy was taken to see the alien bodies from Roswell. Good wrote:

> Around 1961/1962 President J.F. Kennedy expressed a wish to see the alien bodies associated with an alien crash-site. He had obviously been informed of their existence and wished to see for himself the evidence.... According to information received, the alien bodes were taken to Florida when Kennedy went to see them [at] a medical facility."[192]

Support for the claim that Kennedy traveled in 1961 and 1962 to see alien bodies from a UFO crash site comes from a leaked unconfirmed Top Secret CIA Wiretap Summary of conversations involving Marilyn Monroe and the Kennedy brothers. The Wiretap Summary says that Monroe planned to reveal that the President had told her that he had visited an Air Force base that housed UFO and extraterrestrial artifacts:

> [Monroe] had secrets to tell, no doubt arising from her trists [sic] with the President and the Attorney General. One such "secret" mentions the visit by the President at a secret air base for the purpose of inspecting things from outer space.[193]

Monroe died on August 5, 1962 under mysterious circumstances. The next chapter focuses on evidence that her death was related to her plans to blow the whistle on President

Kennedy's secret visit to an Air Force base to see alien bodies, and that Robert Kennedy was directly involved

If the CIA wiretap of Monroe's conversations is accurate, and Monroe was correct in reporting that Kennedy had visited an Air Force base, then this supports Timothy Good's whistleblower who claimed that Kennedy saw alien artifacts at a Florida Air Force facility in 1961/1962. The most likely facility is Homestead Air Force Base. Kennedy made a public visit to Homestead in October, 1962. This was, however, after Monroe's death suggesting that Kennedy had either made an earlier unofficial visit, or visited another Florida Air Force base.

Figure 26. President Kennedy arrives at Homestead Air Force Base – 11/25/1962

Finally, we have the case of President Kennedy visiting the three contiguous military facilities at White Sands Missile Range, Fort Bliss and Holloman Air Force Base on June 6, 1963. Here is how an *El Paso Times* reporter describes the June 6 White Sands visit:

President John F. Kennedy paid the first presidential visit in history here Wednesday, and viewed a flawless, brilliant display of America's missile might... After a brief speech, the Chief Executive boarded a shiny Presidential limousine and, with members of his official party, was driven to two launching sights on the range, where he witnessed – with obvious pleasure – seven missile and rocket firings. President Kennedy flew to White Sands in a five-helicopter convoy from Holloman Air Force Base, N.M. He was accompanied by Vice President Lyndon Johnson, many of the nation's ranking senators and congressmen, top military brass...[194]

As mentioned earlier, White Sands was the base where former Nazi scientists and engineers who were repatriated under Project Paperclip were stationed. From his 1945 Germany tour, Kennedy was familiar with some of the advanced technologies developed by the Nazis. He was also very likely introduced by his mentor, Navy Secretary James Forrestal, to information that some of these technologies were extraterrestrial in origin. If Kennedy wanted to view and be briefed about extraterrestrial technologies, White Sands missile base and the adjoining military facilities were the places to visit.

Timothy Cooper is the individual to whom many of the Majestic documents were originally mailed. A number of these documents have been rigorously checked and shown not to be hoaxes.[195] This gives Cooper and his sources a degree of credibility. According to one of Cooper's reliable sources, when Kennedy traveled to the White Sands facility, he received a tour and a classified UFO briefing.[196] If accurate, this meant that Kennedy asserted his Commander-in-Chief authority to gain access to classified facilities. This may explain why he was accompanied by Vice-President Johnson during the visit, also a first for the American Southwest.[197]

Did Kennedy Receive Messages from and Meet with Extraterrestrials?

Rare first-hand witness evidence that Kennedy had received information about UFOs and extraterrestrial life comes from a former flight steward on Air Force One. Bill Holden claims that Kennedy was aware that UFOs were extraterrestrial in origin. In a June, 2007 interview, Holden explained that in June 1963, while flying to Germany on Air Force One, he placed two newspapers before Kennedy in which UFOs were clearly pictured on the front page. In response to Kennedy's question about what he thought of UFOs, Holden said: "For us to believe that we are the only intelligent beings in the world is unbelievable. So, yes, I believe that there is such a thing as other human species as well as UFOs."[198] In response, President Kennedy said: "You're right, young man." The unqualified nature of Kennedy's response reveals he had knowledge that UFOs did exist, and were interplanetary in origin. More significant was the implication that Kennedy knew some extraterrestrials were human-looking. This leads to the extraordinary claims by George Adamski that President Kennedy received messages from and even met with human-looking extraterrestrials.

Adamski's claims of having filmed flying saucers and meeting with their human-looking extraterrestrial occupants have long been controversial despite supporting photographic, film and eyewitness testimonies. Adamski's famous Desert Center meeting with an extraterrestrial emerging from a "scout ship" on November 20, 1952, was seen by six witnesses who signed affidavits confirming Adamski's version of events.[199] In fact, four of the witnesses immediately reported the incident to a nearby newspaper, the *Phoenix Gazette*, which published the story on November 24 featuring photos and sketches. The Desert Center encounter was among those of Adamski's claims regarding extraterrestrial contact that, according to UFO researcher Timothy Good, were "accurately reported," and "sensible and verifiable".[200]

The testimonies of a number of eyewitnesses and investigators of Adamski give credence to his claims of having secret meetings with European dignitaries including Pope John XXIII and members of the Pentagon to secretly brief them about extraterrestrial life.[201] Among the more controversial of Adamski's claims is that he privately met with President Kennedy in late 1961 and again in 1962. Adamski claims that, during his first visit, he passed on a message from his extraterrestrial contacts about a future world crisis – thought to be the October 1962 Cuban Missile Crisis.

Desmond Leslie, a former Royal Air Force pilot, Irish Lord and cousin to Winston Churchill, closely investigated Adamski's claims. Adamski claimed he secretly visited Pope John XXIII and passed on a message from extraterrestrials to him shortly before the Pope's death - after the completion of the opening session of the Second Vatican Council which lasted from October 11 to December 8, 1962. Leslie was subsequently able to confirm that Adamski did meet Pope John XXIII and was given a papal gold medallion for his service. Leslie consulted his "close friend Cardinal Basel Hume [who] explained that such a medal could not be bought and that Adamski must have done something quite important to have received such a gift."[202]

Adamski's claim of having an ordnance pass, which gave him access to U.S. military facilities, was confirmed by William Sherwood who, at the time, worked at Eastman Kodak as an optical physicist, and Madeline Rodeffer who worked as personal secretary for the U.S. Air Force.[203] Sherwood himself had previously worked for the U.S. Ordnance Department and possessed his own ordnance pass. Both Sherwood and Rodeffer saw Adamski's ordnance pass thereby giving credence to his claims that he secretly briefed the Pentagon about his extraterrestrial contacts.

If Adamski regularly briefed the Pentagon and European VIPs, this would bolster his claim that he secretly met with President Kennedy around October, 1961 to deliver a message from the "space brothers." The message contained advice on a world crisis to occur in about a year that was later revealed to be the October 1962 Cuban Missile Crisis. If true, the contents of the message may have helped Kennedy develop the right strategy for dealing with a conflict that could easily have escalated into a Third World War. The extraterrestrial message, apparently, also contained an invitation for Kennedy to meet with them in California. According to Adamski, President Kennedy accepted the invitation.

Lou Zinstag, the niece of the eminent Swiss psychiatrist Carl Jung, describes what she was told by Adamski concerning Kennedy's alleged meeting with extraterrestrials:

> I still remember his [Adamski's] White House story. He told me that he had been entrusted with a written invitation for President Kennedy to visit one of the space people's huge mother ships at a secret airbase in Desert Hot Springs, California, for few days. In order to keep this visit absolutely secret, Adamski was to take the invitation directly to the White House through a side door. Still glowing with excitement and smiling happily, he explained how the row of cars in which his taxi was traveling had to stop because of a red light just in front of this particular door where a man he knew - a spaceman, he said - was standing ready to let him in. Adamski later learned that Kennedy had spent several hours at the airbase after having canceled an important trip to New York, and that he had a long talk with the ships crew, but that he had not been invited for a flight."[204]

The quality of witness testimonies, photos and film evidence all lead to the conclusion that George Adamski was largely telling the truth about his flying saucer sightings and contacts with human-looking extraterrestrials.[205] There is, however, no reliable independent evidence that Kennedy met with the extraterrestrials that Adamski claims he was in contact with. The only eyewitness testimony related to Adamski's claim, concerns President Kennedy secretly traveling to an undisclosed Air Force base to watch UFOs in flight. A reliable source, according to UFO researcher Timothy Cooper, said that Kennedy "did fly out to an air force base to personally watch an unidentified bogie track from an aircraft under tight security which got no press coverage sometime in 1962."[206] This event appears to be different from Kennedy's visits to view remnants of crashed UFOs and alien bodies. If Kennedy actually traveled to a secret meeting with human-looking extraterrestrials, no one other than Adamski has come forward to say it happened.

Conclusion: Kennedy's CIA End-Run Partly Succeeds

Kennedy partly succeeded in doing an end-run around the CIA's and MJ-12s efforts to deny him access to UFO/extraterrestrial information by receiving secret briefings and visiting various Air Force facilities. The testimonies by Philip Corso, William Holding and anonymous whistleblowers all point to secret meetings, briefings and visits to classified Air Force facilities where President Kennedy learned about extraterrestrial life and technology.

The most surprising information is Adamski's claims that he personally delivered messages from extraterrestrials and arranged for Kennedy to meet aliens at some undisclosed location. While Adamski's claims have been dismissed by many UFO researchers, his claims regarding Kennedy need to be reconsidered in light of new information about Kennedy's efforts to learn about UFOs.

Finally, we need to reconsider events surrounding the death of Marilyn Monroe. Leaked documents and eyewitness reports confirm that she was planning a tell-all press conference that would announce to the world President Kennedy's secret that he had directly witnessed extraterrestrial artifacts at a secret Air Force facility. Monroe's planned tell-all press conference directly jeopardized the Kennedy brothers' efforts to restore direct Presidential oversight of extraterrestrial related issues. The stakes couldn't be higher since President Kennedy had so far been frustrated in his efforts to regain control of UFO information from the CIA. If Monroe blew the whistle, the Kennedys would have had zero chance of learning anything from the secretly appointed officials in charge of extraterrestrial affairs

Endnotes Chapter 7

[190] Grant Cameron, "The Robert Kennedy UFO Story," http://www.presidentialufo.com/old_site/robert_kennedy.htm

[191] Philip Corso with William Birnes, *The Day After Roswell* (Pocket Books, 1997).

[192] Timothy Good, *Need to Know* (Pegasus, 2007) 420-21.

[193] Source: http://majesticdocuments.com/pdf/marilynmonroe.pdf

[194] Source: http://elpasotimes.typepad.com/morgue/2010/07/1963-president-kennedy-views-flawless-white-sands-missile-shots.html

[195] See Stanton Friedman, *Top Secret MAJIC* (Marlowe and Co., 2005)

[196] Source: http://presidentialufo.com/old_site/johnf.htm

[197] Source: http://elpasotimes.typepad.com/morgue/2013/04/1963-over-300000-will-greet-jfk-on-visit-to-el-paso.html

[198] Cited online at: http://projectcamelot.org/bill_holden_interview_transcript.html

[199] Adamski wrote about his encounter in, *The Flying Saucers have Landed* (British Book Center, 1953).

[200] Timothy Good, *Alien Base: The Evidence for Extraterrestrial Colonization of Earth* (Avon Books, 1998) 154-55.

[201] Witness testimonies available in a video available online at: http://youtu.be/kPvvz7O3CKk See also Michael Salla, http://tinyurl.com/oqyjh4e

[202] Neil Gould, "Revisiting George Adamski's claims of Human looking Extraterrestrials," *Exopolitics Journal*, http://exopoliticsjournal.com/vol-3/vol-3-2-Gould.htm

[203] See Neil Gould, "Revisiting George Adamski's claims of Human looking Extraterrestrials," *Exopolitics Journal*, http://exopoliticsjournal.com/vol-3/vol-3-2-Gould.htm Testimonies available in a multiple part video. Part 1 is available online at: http://youtu.be/kPvvz7O3CKk

[204] Cited online at: http://www.presidentialufo.com/johnf.htm

[205] Testimonies and film supporting Adamski's claims are presented in video available online at: http://www.youtube.com/watch?v=kPvvz7O3CKk&feature=channel . See also Neil Gould, "Revisiting George Adamski's claims of Human looking Extraterrestrials," *Exopolitics Journal* 3:2 (July 2009).

[206] Cited online at: http://www.theforbiddenknowledge.com/hardtruth/jfk_ufos.htm

Chapter 8

Marilyn Monroe Death Connected to Kennedy Brothers and UFOs

Introduction

On Saturday, May 19, 1962, Marilyn Monroe, wearing a glittering flesh colored dress, sang Happy Birthday to President John F. Kennedy in front of an audience of 15,000 at the old Madison Square Garden. Afterward Kennedy came up on stage and joked: "I can now retire from politics after having had Happy Birthday sung to me in such a sweet, wholesome way." It was a very public demonstration of Monroe's affection for Kennedy and his appreciation of her talents. The performance, along with Jackie Kennedy's noticeable absence, fueled rumors that Kennedy and Monroe were having an intimate relationship. The only surviving photo of Kennedy and Monroe was taken at a private gathering after the performance – the Secret Service and FBI had a long-standing policy to confiscate any photos of the President with Monroe.

The surviving photo depicts a tense conversation the President is having with Monroe, while his brother, Attorney General, Robert, looks on. On August 5, less than three months later, Monroe was found dead in her apartment. Several eyewitnesses reported seeing Robert Kennedy visit Monroe at her apartment on the day of her death. Did her death have anything to do with her relationship with the President and even his brother? More importantly, did her death have anything to do with alleged pillow talk about sensitive national security issues, including UFOs? Does an unconfirmed CIA document give answers to these questions? Let's begin with how and when Kennedy and Monroe first met.

Figure 27. John and Robert Kennedy having a tense conversation with Marilyn Monroe on May 9, 1962. Source: JFK Presidential Library

The Kennedy Brothers and Marilyn Monroe

A close friend and confidant of Marilyn Monroe was the actor Peter Lawford, who was married to John Kennedy's younger sister, Pat, from 1954 to 1966. According to Lawford's third wife, Deborah Gould, Kennedy first met Monroe during the 1960 Presidential campaign.[207] Around this time, Monroe's marriage to Arthur Miller was ending; they actually divorced several days after Kennedy's Presidential inauguration. The Kennedys threw lavish parties at Lawford's Malibu home. There were ample opportunities for John Kennedy to begin an affair as many claimed occurred. Rachael Bell, who conducted an investigation of Monroe's death for Court TV, explains how the Kennedy brothers met and became intimately involved with Monroe:

> That same year [1960] Marilyn became involved in a highly publicized, but short-lived affair with Frank Sinatra. She also befriended several high-profile personalities during that time, including Peter Lawford, his wife Pat Kennedy, and Pat Newcomb, who became her best friend. The entire group would often spend time together, frequently attending gatherings or large parties at the Lawford and Kennedy homes. The guests were the who's who of Hollywood and at times high government officials would attend, including Robert Kennedy and his brother, then President John Kennedy. According to Tim Coates' *Marilyn Monroe: The F.B.I Files*, it was during these parties that Marilyn and the Kennedy brothers became acquainted during the beginning months of 1962.... Marilyn was often seen dancing or in intimate conversation at private parties with Bobby or John. According to her closest friends, her heart belonged to the elder brother, John. [208]

The testimony of one of his former advisors helps confirm that President Kennedy did indeed have an intimate relationship with Monroe:

> On one occasion they were caught by a former Kennedy advisor, Peter Summers, who saw them come out from the bathroom together. Marilyn was wearing just a towel. Summers was quoted as saying, "She had clearly

been in there, in the shower, with him. It was obvious, but neither of them seemed worried about it."[209]

Rachael Bell, goes on to explain that Monroe formed unrealistic ideas about how her relationship with Kennedy would evolve, and this created danger for the President. Bell cites Lawford as another source confirming the Kennedy-Monroe relationship:

> According to Peter Lawford, Marilyn's unrealistic notions about becoming First Lady caused her to embarrass herself with both Kennedy brothers. Her letters and telephone calls to them had become both tiresome and very risky. It was one thing to cavort with anonymous girls, but quite another to be involved with a celebrity sex symbol like Marilyn Monroe. There was every good reason for JFK and RFK to break off the relationship with Marilyn permanently.[210]

Yet another source revealing Monroe's hopes of becoming First Lady is cited by Bell:

> John spoke frequently to Marilyn on the phone during the beginning to mid 1962. He even gave her a private number so that she could reach him through the Justice Department. Marilyn's hopes for a future with the president began to soar during this time and she believed that he would someday divorce Jackie Kennedy and marry her. Summers states that according to Marilyn's friend, Terry Moore, Marilyn naively "imagined herself as a future First Lady."[211]

The reality of U.S. Presidential politics meant that Kennedy could never hope to be re-elected if he ended his marriage and openly continued his relationship with Monroe. He would eventually have to end the relationship to protect both his Presidency and marriage. Bell explains, however, how dangerous Monroe could be in response to the President's rejection of her:

> What allegedly became so troublesome was Marilyn's supposed rage at JFK's rejection of her and the fear that she was able to strike in both brothers. Donald Wolfe sums it up: "Marilyn Monroe was in a position to bring down the presidency. She was cognizant of Jack Kennedy's marital infidelities and other private matters. She had his notes and letters and was privy to Kennedy's involvement with Sam Giancana. That the Kennedy brothers had discussed national security matters with the film star added to an astonishing array of indiscretions." [212]

Here we have a hint that John Kennedy's indiscretions with Monroe extended to sharing sensitive national security matters. If publicly revealed, this could bring down his Presidency, let alone his sexual indiscretions with Monroe. According to Dr. Donald Burleson, Kennedy was read the riot act by FBI Director Hoover over Monroe being a security risk:

> A few days after the birthday bash, FBI chief J. Edgar Hoover had a conference with Jack Kennedy. It appears that Hoover laid the law down to JFK about the President's having become a security risk due to his intimate association with Marilyn Monroe, who was known to be keeping company with a number of left-wing people ... Hoover seems to have prevailed, because JFK immediately had Marilyn's private line to the White House disconnected. [213]

Figure 28. Hoover meets with President Kennedy and Attorney General Kennedy in Feb 1961. Source: JFK Library

This is when the President's brother, Robert, took a prominent role in the story. President Kennedy decided it would be best to end his relationship with Monroe. Who better to deliver the news to Monroe without her exploding in a fit of rage, and going public with what she knew, than the President's brother, Attorney General, Robert Kennedy? According to Slatzer, "Bobby became the emissary to soothe the fury of the woman scorned."[214]

There were rumors that Monroe also began an affair with Robert Kennedy who in mid-1962 was entrusted with the job of ensuring that Monroe's relationship with his brother ended smoothly, without any damaging press leaks. Dr. Susan Doll explains some of the sources and their credibility:

> Speculation on Marilyn's affair with Robert Kennedy is based on numerous eyewitness reports of their meetings together, particularly at Peter Lawford's beachfront home in Malibu. However, specific facts regarding their relationship are even more scarce than those involving Marilyn and JFK. Details conflict and versions of the same

anecdotes are contradictory…. What does remain difficult to discount is that Marilyn made repeated phone calls to the Justice Department -- where Attorney General Robert Kennedy worked -- shortly after she was fired by Fox.[215]

Slatzer was an important source for the Bobby-Marilyn relationship, claiming she had confided in him during their last meeting, two days before her death:

> When I last saw her she confided to me that Bobby had only recently tried to sever their relationship as well. Like Jack, Bobby offered no explanation.[216]

Regarding the alleged relationship between Robert Kennedy and Marilyn Monroe, William Sullivan, Hoover's Deputy Director of the FBI, claims there is no evidence that a sexual encounter ever happened. In his autobiography, *The Bureau: My Thirty Years in Hoover's FBI* (1979), he writes:

> Although Hoover was desperately trying to catch Bobby Kennedy red-handed at anything, he never did. Kennedy was almost a Puritan. We used to watch him at parties, where he would order one glass of scotch and still be sipping from the same glass two hours later. The stories about Bobby Kennedy and Marilyn Monroe were just stories. The original story was invented by a so-called journalist, a right-wing zealot who had a history of spinning wild yarns. It spread like wildfire, of course, and J. Edgar Hoover was right there, gleefully fanning the flames.[217]

So while stories of a relationship between Robert Kennedy and Monroe are still disputed, Monroe's repeated calls to the Justice

Department, which Robert Kennedy headed, suggest that he was trying to prevent Monroe from going public with her relationship with his brother. Did she threaten to go public and reveal her affair with the President? Is there any truth to rumors of a "tell all" press conference where she was going to reveal the contents of her "red diary"?

Monroe Plans Tell All Press Conference with Red Diary

According to Donald Burleson:

> In the end, Marilyn felt rejected by both Kennedy brothers, and with good reason. Like JFK, Bobby … made himself inaccessible to Marilyn by phone. The Kennedys had dropped her, distanced themselves from her. She was furious with them, and during the final two or three days of her life she began telling close friends that she might just hold a news conference and "tell all".[218]

One of the many people who spoke with Monroe on her final day was a male companion from Mexico who managed to befriend her. Reporter Greg Brian, a freelance writer of a number of Monroe articles, explains:

> One key figure in proof toward the idea that Marilyn was going to give a press conference was a fan from Mexico, Jose Bolanos, who somehow managed to befriend (or become a new lover to) Marilyn when she visited Mexico earlier in the year. He kept in contact with her often and was one of the many friends who talked to her via phone on that final day of her life. Marilyn reportedly told Bolanos that she knew a lot of powerful things from the Kennedys and would soon reveal something that would "shock the world." That comment has been more or less

considered to be true, which means Marilyn had to know things she shouldn't have.[219]

In a 1993 documentary, one of Monroe's former lovers (and husband for a day) Robert Slatzer said that Monroe, two days before her death, told him:

> If I don't hear from Bobby Kennedy before the end of the weekend, I'm going to call a press conference, and blow the lid off this whole _____ thing! ... I'm going to tell about my relationship with both Kennedy brothers. Everybody has been calling, trying to get the story anyway----Walter Winchell, Kilgallen. And it's clear to me now that the Kennedys got what they wanted out of me and then moved on."[220]

According to Slatzer, Monroe also told Jeanne Carmen and Elizabeth Courtney that she was planning a press conference the following Monday, Aug. 6, 1962. Monroe planned to reveal secrets recorded in an alleged red diary. Did it really exist?

According to a number of Monroe's close friends and the advice of her doctor, she kept a personal diary. In it, she recorded many details of her activities, most noteworthy being her meetings with the Kennedy brothers. The diary's existence has been called into question since it was allegedly never found after her death. Yet a number of witnesses have confirmed personally seeing it, that it did contain many disturbing secrets, and it was eventually retrieved by the LA police but kept hidden.

One of those who saw the diary was Slatzer who revealed, in an interview with Donald Wolfe, what Monroe had told and showed him at their last meeting:

> What Marilyn revealed to me that day on the beach, I found deeply disturbing," Slatzer confides. She removed

her small red diary from her bag and showed Slatzer her "book of secrets." "What is it?" Slatzer asked. It's my diary, she replied. "I want you to look through it." Slatzer remembers thumbing through the pages and finding notes of her conversations with the Kennedys....Slatzer said he asked her why she had made the notations. "Mostly because Bobby liked to talk about political things," she replied. I wanted to be able to talk about things he was interested in."[221]

Donald Wolfe has done the most research in tracking down witnesses who knew of or had seen Monroe's diary. Wolfe said that in addition to Slatzer, another of Monroe's friends, Lionel Grandison, had seen the diary and looked through its contents.[222]

Another witness was former Los Angeles Police Department intelligence officer, Mike Rothmiller. In an interview with Wolfe, Rothmiller claimed that in 1978, he saw the Marilyn Monroe file which included a copy of her diary which he examined:

It was more like a journal... The majority of the entries were notes about conversations Marilyn Monroe had with John F. Kennedy and Robert Kennedy. The subject matter ranged from Russia and Cuba to the Mafia and Sinatra. I remember she referred to Castro as Fidel C.[223]

Finally, Norman Jefferies claims that he also saw Monroe's red diary, which she kept in her bedroom or locked in a file cabinet in the guest cottage. After Monroe's death, his mother-in-law, Eunice Murray, handed the diary over to the Coroner's office.

In summary, according to multiple witnesses, Monroe did keep a red diary, which contained notes of her private conversations with the Kennedy brothers. If Monroe decided to go public about her affairs with Jack and Bobby Kennedy, she could offer the diary's contents as evidence supporting her claims. The diary's existence and its contents could bring an end to the Kennedy administration. It provided a powerful motive for Robert Kennedy to see Monroe one last time and appeal to her to surrender the diary and remain quiet about her Kennedy liaisons.

Robert Kennedy Searches for Monroe's Red Diary

This takes us to the final day of Monroe's life. Independent eyewitnesses reported seeing Robert Kennedy accompanied by two men enter Monroe's apartment on two occasions. According to Rachel Bell: "there are some witnesses, including a cop, who place Robert Kennedy near the scene that night."[224]

Greg Brian also reports that a number of police and an FBI informant saw Robert Kennedy in Los Angeles the night of Monroe's death:

> Close friends of RFK say that he was in San Francisco that day with his wife and kids to visit a group of friends on a ranch in the Santa Cruz Mountains. They say he couldn't have been in Los Angeles at the time he was reported to be there. But memory can be deceptive in many people as we all know. When a security risk is imminent--the Attorney General may very well find a way to get there at all costs. Also, when several police officers (plus an FBI informant) claim to have seen RFK in L.A. during the early evening, it moves the possibility of him being there a tad beyond half-truth.[225]

Britain's Independent newspaper reported that Robert Kennedy had visited Monroe that day to threaten her:

Sydney Guilaroff, Marilyn's hairdresser, says Monroe called him twice, quite hysterical, to say that Kennedy had been at her house with Lawford threatening her. The last phone call Monroe made was to the White House. Was she calling JFK? There are even rumors that she spoke to his wife, Jackie.[226]

According to a book by Dr. Burleson, audio surveillance captured Robert Kennedy's voice in the late afternoon having an argument with Monroe. Kennedy was accompanied by his brother-in-law Peter Lawford, and was looking for something. Kennedy became increasingly strident according to Burleson's description of his voice:

> "Where is it? Where the f___ is it?" and things to that effect, "My family must have it," and "We'll make any arrangements you want," and "We'll pay you for it." In retrospect, it's obvious that Bobby was looking for Marilyn's diary.[227]

Eventual Confirmations of Kennedy Visits

Most important was the eventual admission by Monroe's housekeeper, Eunice Murray, in 1985, more than 20 years after Monroe's death, that Robert Kennedy had been at Monroe's house on the day of her death. She made the admission AFTER the end of an interview conducted by Anthony Summers, who was doing a BBC documentary on Monroe's death. For years, Murray had denied the rumors that Kennedy had visited Monroe on her final day. Fortunately, Murray's comments were captured on tape and played during the documentary "Goddess" which aired in Britain, but not in the US!. This is how Summers recalled the extraordinary admission by Murray:

"As the camera crew were starting to clear up, she said suddenly, "why at my age, do I still have to cover up this thing?"

I asked her what she meant, and then she astonished us by admitting that Robert Kennedy was indeed at Marilyn's house the day she died, and that a doctor and an ambulance had come while she was still alive.."

Mrs. Murray then was asked about Kennedy- Monroe relationship.

Murray: Well , over a period of time I was not at all surprised that the Kennedys were a very important part of Marilyn's life...and eh....so that I was just a...I wasn't included in this information, but I was a witness to what was happening...

SUMMERS: And you believe the he (Bobby) was there that day?

MURRAY: At Marilyn's house?

SUMMERS: Yes.

MURRAY: Oh, sure!

SUMMERS: That afternoon?

MURRAY: Yes.

SUMMERS: And you think that is the reason she was so upset?

MURRAY: Yes, and it became so sticky that the protectors of Robert Kennedy, you know, had to step in and protect him...

When Summers asked Murray why she hadn't told the truth to the police in 1962, she responded, " I told whatever I thought was good to tell." [228]

Murray's admission was later supported by her son-in-law, Norman Jeffries, who worked as a handyman for Monroe but strangely was not questioned by police or the media. According to Summers, who tried to contact Jefferies through Eunice Murray when doing his Goddess documentary in 1985, "Murray seemed oddly reluctant to assist me in reaching Jefferies."[229] Summers finally tracked Jefferies down for his documentary, and got him to reveal some details about the Saturday morning when he was known to be working at Monroe's home, but said nothing about the events he witnessed on Saturday night.

In 1992, thirty years after Monroe's death, Jeffries was tracked down once again by another researcher, Donald Wolfe. He had been threatened to keep silent, but now confined to a wheelchair and terminally ill, Jefferies decided he had nothing to lose and revealed to Wolfe that he had worked ALL the day of her death and witnessed ALL the major events. In his interview with Wolfe, included in the latter's book, *The Final Days of Marilyn Monroe*, Jefferies revealed much:

> "I guess they can very well electrocute me in a wheelchair," Jeffries disclosed that he never left the proximity of the Monroe residence on the horrible day. He had remained with his mother in law the entire day from the time he arrived on Saturday at eight o'clock that morning until he departed Sunday morning at approximately seven thirty . He had been present during ALL events that took place.

> " I was there in the living room with Eunice when Marilyn died, and after that all hell broke loose," Jefferies stated.

> He was there when Bobby Kennedy (Robert) And Peter Lawford arrived on Saturday afternoon . He was there when the Ambulance arrived on Saturday Night. He was there when Dr. Greenson arrived and Marilyn Died in the guest Cottage. He was there in the early hours of Sunday

morning when Monroe's body was moved to the bedroom. Norman Jefferies had been a key witness.[230]

Jefferies went into more detail about Kennedy's visit according to Wolfe:

> Norman Jefferies recalled that between 9:30 and 10 P.M., Robert Kennedy, accompanied by two men, appeared at the door. They ordered Jefferies and Murray from the house. 'We were told to leave. I mean they made it clear we were to be gone. We went to a neighbor's house. I had no idea what was going on. I mean, this was the attorney general of the United States. I didn't know who the two men were with him...at about ten-thirty Murray and Jefferies saw Bobby and the two men leave.

> Jefferies stated that he and Murray then ventured back to Marilyn's. As they entered the open gates and crossed the courtyard toward the kitchen door, they heard Maf barking from the guest cottage, where the light was on and the door was standing open. When they entered the cottage, they discovered Marilyn, unclothed, lying across the daybed." He said it didn't look like she was breathing and her color was awful---like she was dead....

> According to Jefferies, at one time 12305 Helena Dr. was swarming with at least a dozen plainclothes officers--- then suddenly they were gone. He had no idea who they were. The officer in charge was later identified by Billy Woodfield and several former LAPD officers as Bobby Kennedy's friend Captain James Hamilton of the LAPD's Intelligence Division, and the two men who had accompanied Bobby Kennedy to MM's house that night

were identified as two detectives assigned to Kennedy as security officers. [231]

Wolfe concluded that Monroe's death was premeditated murder:

> Did they intend to murder MM? Or was the intent to subdue her with a 'hot shot' if she caused any problems while they broke into her file cabinet in the guest cottage; took the notes, letters, and legal documents; and searched for the book of secrets? The evidence points to premeditated homicide. In the presence of Bobby Kennedy, she was injected with enough barbiturate to kill fifteen people."[232]

Jefferies died in 1993, Wolfe was the only Monroe researcher ever to get the truth from Jefferies.

Based on the number of witnesses who have come forward, what becomes clear is that Monroe was planning a "tell all" press conference using notes from her red diary to spite the Kennedy's for their treatment of her. To prevent Monroe moving forward, Robert Kennedy along with accomplices visited Monroe twice on Saturday August 4, once in the afternoon and once in the evening around 9:30 pm. Not heeding the warning given in the afternoon visit to keep silent and surrender her diary, Kennedy returned that night to forcibly remove the red diary from Monroe's possession. In what appeared to be a botched attempt to medicate her, so as to make her pliable, Monroe died. That's when chaos ensued. The doctor and ambulance summoned to revive her were unsuccessful. Eunice Murray and Norman Jefferies were threatened to keep silent about what they had witnessed, and make up a false story for police.

So finally we move to the question of what was Monroe planning to reveal in the aborted "tell all" press conference. The truth about her relationship with the Kennedy brothers would have been the number one item, but what sensitive national security issue was she going to share? It's worth recalling that FBI Director Hoover had warned the President about Monroe being a security threat, and to break off his relationship. So what had she been told? Speculation has focused about the President's plans to assassinate Castro, which on its own would have been a very damaging national security leak. There was however, another national security issue that was apparently even more sensitive than the plan to assassinate Castro. Kennedy had revealed to Monroe classified information about UFOs and extraterrestrial life.

Monroe Knew about the Kennedys' UFO Secrets

The main source for the Monroe-Kennedy UFO link is an alleged CIA document 'leaked' in 1994 summarizing wiretaps of conversations between Dorothy Kilgallen (one of Monroe's confidants) and Howard Rothberg, and between Monroe and Robert Kennedy.[233] An image of the document is on the next page, and is followed by a transcript.

The CIA wiretap refers to "the visit by the President at a secret air base for the purpose of inspecting things from outer space." In the previous chapter, I discussed evidence that the President traveled to various Air Force bases to find out what he could about extraterrestrial life and technology. After being denied direct access by the CIA Director/MJ-12 Group to extraterrestrial secrets, Kennedy tried to educate himself. As Commander in Chief, he had the necessary authority to visit classified facilities at any military base he thought harbored the secrets he was seeking.

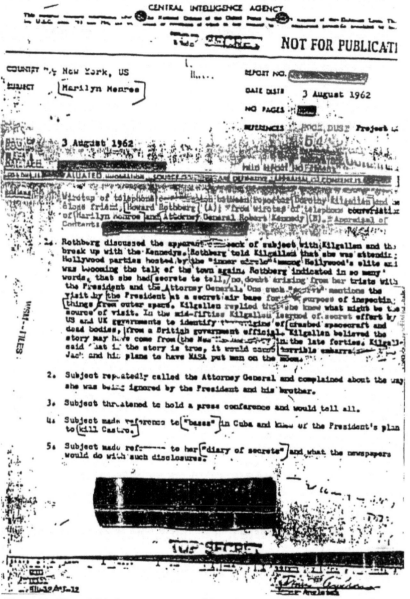

Figure 29. Alleged CIA document summarizing wiretaps of Marilyn Monroe. Source: Majestic Documents

Wiretape of telephone conversation between reporter Dorothy Kilgallen and her close friend, Howard Rothberg (A); from wiretap of telephone conversation of Marilyn Monroe and Attorney General Robert Kennedy (B). Appraisal of Content: *[A portion redacted.]*

1. Rothberg discussed the apparent comeback of subject with Kilgallen and the break up with the Kennedys. Rothberg told Kilgallen that she was attending Hollywood parties hosted by the "inner circle" among Hollywood's elite and was becoming the talk of the town again. Rothberg indicated in so many words, that she had secrets to tell, no doubt arising from her trists *[sic]* with the President and the Attorney General. One such "secret" mentions the visit by the President at a secret air base for the purpose of inspecting things from outer space. Kilgallen replied that she knew what might be the source of visit. In the mid-fifties Kilgallen learned of secret effort by US and UK governments to identify the origins of crashed spacecraft and dead bodies, from a British government official. Kilgallen believed the story may have come from the New Mexico story in the late forties. Kilgallen said that if the story is true, it would cause terrible embarrassment for Jack and his plans to have NASA put men on the moon.

2. Subject repeatedly called the Attorney General and complained about the way she was being ignored by the President and his brother.

3. Subject threatened to hold a press conference and would tell all.

4. Subject made reference to "bases" in Cuba and knew of the President's plan to kill Castro.

5. Subject made reference to her "diary of secrets" and what the newspapers would do with such disclosures.

Figure 30. Transcript of CIA Wiretap Summary

As to what secrets he was seeking in his visits to Air Force facilities, Kilgallen's wiretapped comments are significant:

> Kilgallen replied that she knew what might be the source of visit. In the mid-fifties Kilgallen learned of secret effort by US and UK governments to identify the origins of crashed spacecraft and dead bodies, from a British government official. Kilgallen believed the story may have come from the New Mexico story in the late forties.

The New Mexico story from the late forties she was referring to was either the July, 1947 Roswell "flying saucer" crash that had been covered in several major newspapers, or the Frank Scully book titled *Behind the Flying Saucers* about the 1948 Flying Saucer crash at Aztec, New Mexico. While both incidents were debunked at the time by the mainstream media, subsequent research has found compelling evidence that both crashes occurred as originally claimed.

We can infer from the wiretap that Kennedy was successful with his visits to military facilities to find extraterrestrial secrets. He had learned about one or both of the Roswell (1947) or Aztec (1948) flying saucer crashes, and revealed what he had found to Monroe.

Most important is the wiretap's claim that Monroe "threatened to hold a press conference and would tell all." She referred also to her "diary of secrets," and talked about "what the newspapers would do with such disclosures." Clearly, if authentic, the CIA wiretap document is a smoking gun revealing that Marilyn Monroe knew secrets that threatened to derail the Kennedy administration. Importantly, the wiretap reveals that Monroe was under CIA surveillance, and it could intervene if Monroe threatened to reveal any UFO secrets.

This naturally leads to the question, is the wiretap document authentic? The first thing to consider is that it is a *leaked* document, rather than an officially released document. That means we need to be careful to rule out deception. The time of its release places it among the Majestic Documents, a trove of alleged official documents leaked by various insider sources beginning in 1984.

Is the CIA Wiretap Document Authentic?

In his book, *Extraterrestrial Contact: The Evidence and Implications,* Dr. Steven Greer claims the Monroe CIA wiretap document came to him in 1994. According to Greer, it was "by way of a contact with access to NSA officials."[234] He claimed the wiretap document, "has been authenticated by the best document researcher in the world - a man who for years sat outside General Odom's door as his senior aide when Odom was NSA head."[235] William Odom was Director of the National Security Agency from 1985 to 1989. Greer has gone on the public record to claim that the wiretap document is authentic, and is "smoking gun" proof of a UFO connection to Monroe's death.[236]

Greer went on to point out the significance of one of the names that appears on the wiretap document:

> The reader will note that the document is signed by James Angleton, one of the main CIA counter-intelligence figures of the 1960s and fanatical "mole hunter" who ruthlessly tried to stop any leaks of sensitive intelligence.[237]

An anonymous source known as S-1 claims to have been a retired CIA counterintelligence officer who worked with James Jesus Angleton, who headed the CIA's counter intelligence division. In an unsigned letter, S-1 claims to have retrieved a number of Majestic documents from Angleton's archive after his death in 1987.[238] The most important was the burned memo discussed in chapter 5. As the CIA chief of counter intelligence, Angleton was certainly someone who was in the loop on the most classified national security secrets – including extraterrestrial life. It's plausible that, after his retirement in 1975, Angleton kept a record of documents that detailed his work for future reference. Angleton's documents had to be located and hidden or destroyed after his death. That is why it is plausible that a former co-worker, familiar with their contents, would be given the responsibility to find and destroy them.

According to S-1, his job was to do precisely that. After locating Angleton's documents, apparently he did not follow through on his instructions to destroy them. He decided to leak them instead to Cooper. In his cover letter he states that the documents would establish a link between JFK's death and MJ-12.[239]

Angleton's name appears in the Monroe wiretap. This is significant, since it shows that he was an important authority for monitoring the UFO issue in order to maintain secrecy. It is also logical since Angleton was responsible for CIA counterintelligence. Monroe's associations with Soviet bloc supporters made her a security threat who needed to be monitored, due to the sensitivity of the information the Kennedy brothers shared with her.

There is another name on the wiretap that strongly points to its authenticity. Burleson used computer imaging techniques to enhance the CIA wiretap document and found an imprint of "Gen. Shulgen" next to the "Top Secret" stamp at the top of document. [240]

Figure 31. Burleson's computer enhanced version reveals name of Gen Shulgen.
Source: Majestic Documents

Brigadier General George Shulgen was chief of the Air Intelligence Requirements Division of the U.S. Air Force. Even more intriguing is the imprint's reference to a little-known document known as the "Intelligence Collection Memorandum" that was drafted by Shulgen in October 1947. The "Intelligence Collection Memorandum" contains a list of the "intelligence requirements in the field of Flying Saucer type aircraft."[241] The famous Nathan Twining Memo in which he claimed the flying saucer "phenomenon is something real and not visionary or fictitious" was addressed to Shulgen.[242] This leads to an important conclusion drawn by Burleson:

> This imprint or "bleed-in," however it came to be on a CIA document about Marilyn Monroe, makes a clear connection between her murder and the question of UFO secrecy, as someone, somewhere at some time, evidently thought it logical to archive the documents together.[243]

Shulgen's involvement in the investigation of flying saucers/UFOs, not only helps authenticate the wiretap document, but makes an important connection between the CIA's surveillance of Monroe and the UFO phenomenon.

181

Finally, in his book, *UFOs and the Murder of Marilyn Monroe*, Burleson explains the significance of another name that appeared on the wiretap document. This involved the project Moon Dust which, for years, the U.S. Air Force and other government agencies denied existed.[244] FOIA releases finally succeeded in proving the existence of Project Moon Dust and that it first became operational in the retrieval of space debris in 1953. For example, a Department of Defense document discusses a UFO sighting and its relevance for Project Moon Dust:

> ...this sighting demonstrates a high level of local interest in the subject of UFOs and presages future reporting which could be valuable in pursuit of Project MOON DUST.[245]

The key individual in these FOIA releases was U.S. Army Staff Sergeant Clifford Stone. He began making FOIA requests in the late 1970s while still on active military service.[246] Stone claims that during his entire 22-year military career, he served in an elite UFO crash recovery team that was part of Project Moon Dust.[247] Project Moon Dust, as Burleson points out in his book:

> ... has existed at least since 1953, for the purpose of recovering debris from fallen space vehicles, certainly to include UFO crash debris. An intriguing and problematical project line, certainly, to find on a CIA document about Marilyn Monroe.[248]

The confirmed existence of Project Moon Dust as a one-time operational space debris/UFO retrieval program - once officially denied to exist - helps authenticate the CIA Monroe wiretap.

In summary, we have multiple sources and documentation that help authenticate the CIA Monroe wiretap.

Greer's confidential NSA source claims it is a genuine document. Names such as James Angleton and General Schulgen, that appear on the wiretap memo, have each been shown to have a firm relevance to the UFO issue. Finally, the mention of Project Moon Dust, a top secret UFO retrieval program, also reveals a firm UFO connection. Altogether, this not only helps authenticate the Monroe document, but shows that Monroe had been informed by Kennedy about some of what he had learned about UFOs retrieved and stored at various U.S. military facilities.

Conclusion: Monroe Becomes a Victim of the UFO Cover-Up

President Kennedy revealed to Marilyn Monroe that he had personally witnessed extraterrestrial artifacts at one or more classified military facilities. This was a monumental breach of national security protocol by the President. He was clearly confident, at the time, that Monroe would keep the secrets he was revealing. Monroe summarized all that she had been told in a "Red Diary". FBI Director Hoover first warned the President and then Robert Kennedy about Monroe's political affiliations, and that she was a security threat. Hoover insisted that the Kennedy brothers terminate their personal relationships with her. Monroe was furious and planned a tell-all press conference. The responsibility fell to Robert Kennedy to stop her. In desperation, he visited her twice on the day of her death.

On the first occasion, traveling with Peter Lawford, Robert Kennedy failed to persuade Monroe to abandon her plan. Later that night, Kennedy went back with a doctor and another agent. The plan was to retrieve the diary and to silence Monroe. It is highly unlikely that Robert Kennedy would have been physically present at Monroe's residence, if the plan was to search her premises and murder her as claimed by Donald Wolfe.[249] A more plausible scenario is that Kennedy thought that Monroe would be medicated by one of the agents while he and the other searched Monroe's premises. The agent/doctor administering the medication either botched the dosage, or, unknown to Kennedy, had been instructed to administer a lethal dosage. If the latter scenario is closer to the truth, then it is feasible that the CIA counterintelligence surveillance team monitoring Monroe arranged for one of its agents to infiltrate the Los Angeles police intelligence team assisting Kennedy. The premeditated murder would enable CIA's counterintelligence division to make it look as though Kennedy was involved in a botched attempt to silence Monroe. Angleton could use Monroe's death and Kennedy's involvement as future leverage against the Attorney General.

We will never be certain whether her death was a botched attempt by Robert Kennedy to silence her, or a premeditated murder by CIA counterintelligence who framed the U.S. Attorney General. The truth about her death was never released due to the cover up request by Kennedy to the chief of the Special Division of the Los Angeles Police Department. The two eyewitnesses to the events that fateful night, Murray and Jefferies, were intimidated into silence.

Most importantly, the leaked CIA document is evidence that Angleton had wiretapped Monroe's phones and was monitoring the extent of her knowledge of the UFO/extraterrestrial phenomenon. As chief of counterintelligence, Angleton would have been directly interested in Monroe's association with Socialist supporters who could pass on sensitive information to the Soviet bloc. As the CIA gatekeeper for UFO/extraterrestrial information, Angleton was probably monitoring Monroe's knowledge of what the President had told her. One of the secrets she planned to share in her tell-all press conference was that Kennedy had visited Air Force facilities to view UFO artifacts. Apparently, the President had succeeded in his end-run around the CIA to learn about UFOs and extraterrestrial life using his power as Commander-in-Chief.

Unfortunately, Kennedy's indiscretion in sharing what he saw ultimately had tragic consequences. Monroe became the first high profile victim of the UFO cover-up in the Kennedy administration. She would not be the last.

Endnotes - Chapter 8

[207] See Susan Doll, Ph.D., "Marilyn Monroe's Final Years," http://entertainment.howstuffworks.com/marilyn-monroe-final-years6.htm

[208] Source: http://tinyurl.com/lvuxyx5

[209] Source: http://tinyurl.com/lvuxyx5

[210] Source: http://tinyurl.com/8a9awr

[211] Source: http://tinyurl.com/lvuxyx5

[212] Source: http://tinyurl.com/8a9awr

[213] Donald Burleson, *UFOs and the Murder of Marilyn Monroe* (Black Mesa Press, 2003) p. 28-29. See also Wolfe, *The Last Days of Marilyn Monroe*, p. 59.

[214] Donald Wolfe, *The Last Days of Marilyn Monroe*, 60.

[215] Source: http://entertainment.howstuffworks.com/marilyn-monroe-final-years7.htm

[216] Donald Wolfe, *The Last Days of Marilyn Monroe*, 60.

[217] Source: http://tinyurl.com/pcsjueo

[218] Burleon, *UFOs and the Murder of Marilyn Monroe*, 29-30

[219] Source: http://tinyurl.com/q54rher

[220] Peter Harry Brown, *Marilyn Monroe - The Last Take* (Signet, 1993) 299

[221] Donald Wolfe, *The Last Days of Marilyn Monroe*, 60.

[222] Donald Wolfe, *The Last Days of Marilyn Monroe*, 36.

[223] Donald Wolfe, *The Last Days of Marilyn Monroe*, 36.

[224] Source: http://tinyurl.com/omxfyqx

[225] Source: http://tinyurl.com/q54rher

[226] Source: http://tinyurl.com/oeczxb9

[227] Donald Burleson, *UFOs and the Murder of Marilyn Monroe*, 33

[228] Source: http://www.angelfire.com/stars/mmgoddess/MURRAY.html

[229] Source: http://www.angelfire.com/stars/mmgoddess/JEFFERIES.html

[230] Source: http://www.angelfire.com/stars/mmgoddess/JEFFERIES.html

[231] Donald Wolfe, *The Last Days of Marilyn Monroe*, 462-463.

[232] Donald Wolfe, *The Last Days of Marilyn Monroe*, 462-463.

[233] Available online at: http://majesticdocuments.com/pdf/marilynmonroe.pdf

[234] Steven Greer, *Extraterrestrial Contact: The Evidence and Implications* (Crossing Point Inc, 1999). Extract available online at: http://tinyurl.com/2f7cdrg

[235] Steven Greer, *Extraterrestrial Contact: The Evidence and Implications*. Extract available online at: http://tinyurl.com/2f7cdrg

[236] Steven Greer, *Extraterrestrial Contact: The Evidence and Implications*. Extract available online at: http://tinyurl.com/2f7cdrg

[237] Steven Greer, *Extraterrestrial Contact: The Evidence and Implications*. Extract available online at: http://tinyurl.com/2f7cdrg

[238] http://majesticdocuments.com/pdf/burnedmemocoverletter.pdf

[239] Source: http://majesticdocuments.com/pdf/burnedmemocoverletter.pdf

[240] See: http://www.blackmesapress.com/page4.htm

[241] Available online at: http://www.project1947.com/fig/schulgen.htm

[242] http://www.roswellfiles.com/FOIA/twining.htm

[243] Source: http://www.blackmesapress.com/page4.htm

[244] See Burleson, *UFOs and the Murder of Marilyn Monroe*, 58.

[245] Source: http://www.majesticdocuments.com/pdf/moondust_morocco_18jan67.pdf

[246] See Michael Salla, "The Covert World of UFO Crash Retrievals - An Overview of Personnel Management in Majestic-12 Group Projects," *Exopolitics Journal* http://exopoliticsjournal.com/vol-2/vol-2-2-Salla.htm#_ednref12

[247] Stone provides documentary evidence for the existence of Project Moondust in his book, Clifford Stone, *UFOs Are Real: Extraterrestrial Encounters Documented by the U.S. Government* (SPI Books, 1997).

[248] Burleson, *UFOs and the Murder of Marilyn Monroe*, 58.

[249] Donald Wolfe, *The Last Days of Marilyn Monroe*, 463

Chapter 9

Kennedy's Attempt to Cooperate with the USSR on Space and UFOs

Introduction

In his Inaugural Address on January 20, 1961, President Kennedy indirectly referred to President Eisenhower's farewell speech warning about the growing power of the military-industrial complex. Kennedy described the dangers posed by the armaments industry using science to build ever more destructive weapons:

> Finally, to those nations who would make themselves our adversary, we offer not a pledge but a request: that both sides begin anew the quest for peace, before the dark powers of destruction unleashed by science engulf all humanity in planned or accidental self-destruction.
>
> We dare not tempt them with weakness. For only when our arms are sufficient beyond doubt can we be certain beyond doubt that they will never be employed. But neither can two great and powerful groups of nations take comfort from our present course -- both sides overburdened by the cost of modern weapons, both rightly alarmed by the steady spread of the deadly atom, yet both racing to alter that uncertain balance of terror that stays the hand of mankind's final war....[250]

Kennedy went on to make a bold appeal for cooperation with the Soviet Union in arms control, science and the exploration of space:

> Let both sides, for the first time, formulate serious and precise proposals for the inspection and control of arms, and bring the absolute power to destroy other nations under the absolute control of all nations. Let both sides seek to invoke the wonders of science instead of its terrors.[251]

It was Kennedy's appeal for joint cooperation in space with the Soviet Union that was the most important clue to his intention to regain control of the UFO issue. During his administration, Kennedy would repeatedly reach out to the Soviet Union to cooperate in space, along with a host of other areas of mutual concern:

> Together let us explore the stars, conquer the deserts, eradicate disease, tap the ocean depths, and encourage the arts and commerce... And, if a beachhead of cooperation may push back the jungle of suspicion, let both sides join in creating a new endeavor -- not a new balance of power, but a new world of law -- where the strong are just, and the weak secure, and the peace preserved.[252]

If cooperation with the Soviet Union were to be established in the international arena, then it would significantly reduce the power of the military-industrial complex. More importantly, cooperation with the Soviet Union would undercut the power of the secretive group that had gained exclusive control over the UFO issue, and were using extraterrestrial-related technologies for weapons development.

Kennedy's outreach to the Soviet Union and its leader, Nikita Khrushchev, would eventually bear fruit in the last months of his presidency, but not without much confrontation and crisis in the intervening period. Kennedy's first goal with the Soviet Union was to build the foundations for cooperation and peaceful relations in a number of international areas. On February 22, 1961, Kennedy would write the first of a series of letters to Khrushchev pledging cooperation in areas of disagreement, finding peaceful solutions to world problems, and requesting a meeting to promote these ends. In his first, Kennedy wrote:

> I am sure that you are as conscious as I am of the heavy responsibility which rests upon our two Governments in world affairs. I agree with your thought that if we could find a measure of cooperation on some of these current issues this, in itself, would be a significant contribution to the problem of insuring a peaceful and orderly world…. I hope it will be possible, before too long, for us to meet personally for an informal exchange of views in regard to some of these matters…. I hope such exchanges might assist us in working out a responsible approach to our differences with the view to their ultimate resolution for the benefit of peace and security throughout the world. You may be sure, Mr Chairman, that I intend to do everything I can toward developing a more harmonious relationship between our two countries.[253]

Kennedy's overture to Khrushchev for world peace and harmony was soon eclipsed by the international crisis stemming from a covert operation manufactured by the CIA and its Director, Allen Dulles. The covert operation involved an invasion of Cuba by approximately 2000 Cuban exiles that would establish a beachhead, and then call for international recognition and assistance for 'liberated' Cuban territory. Kennedy was briefed on the plan by Dulles, and was told that it had been approved by President Eisenhower himself. Dulles was confident that the plan would succeed and explained the detailed preparations behind it. Kennedy felt obliged to follow through on the plan despite his own reservations. He laid down strict conditions limiting overt U.S. military involvement. The U.S. military would not be involved in openly fighting Cuban forces during the "invasion," and could only intervene once the Cuban exiles had established their beachhead and expanded into Cuban territory. Kennedy denied air cover to the operation.

On April 17, 1961, the covert operation went ahead. It was badly executed and became known as the Bay of Pigs fiasco. The botched operation immediately led to tension between the Kennedy Administration and the Soviet Union. Kennedy was furious at Dulles, who now knew that his time as Director of the CIA was now limited. He would in fact resign in November, 1961; but not before he had secretly set in place a set of MJ-12 directives that would stymie President Kennedy's efforts to learn more about the mysterious UFO phenomenon.

On April 22, Kennedy had another meeting with President Eisenhower, this time at Camp David, Maryland. According to the official agenda, the topic was Cuba. Eisenhower had plenty of advice to share in their private conversation. The public would learn that Eisenhower admonished Kennedy for refusing to give air cover to the CIA operation. Once the covert operation had been approved, it was necessary to ensure success, even if that meant openly committing U.S. forces. That is what the public was told about their private discussion. What did they really discuss?

High on the agenda was the way in which covert operations were being run by the CIA and the impact these were having on international affairs. The failed Cuba invasion was the tip of the iceberg. The CIA had to be reined in, but how to do it? At the same time, how could Kennedy find out about the secret operations concerning UFOs that he had partially learned about from his own wartime experiences, his time in Congress, and earlier meetings with Eisenhower?

Figure 32. Kennedy meets Eisenhower at Camp David, April 22, 1961. Source: JFK Presidential Library

Kennedy began by implementing reforms on how covert operations were being run. Oversight would be transferred from the CIA to the Pentagon. In chapter 5, I discussed Kennedy's three National Security Action Memoranda (NSAM) issued on June 28, 1961 to place covert CIA operations under the control of the Joint Chiefs of Staff.[254]

Khrushchev finally replied to Kennedy's February 22nd letter on May 12, 1961, only weeks after the Bay of Pigs fiasco. Khrushchev acknowledged the mutual desire for peaceful relations:

> We share the ideas expressed by you ... concerning the necessity of avoiding dangerous complications which

create a threat to peace and of ensuring peaceful coexistence and the peaceful development of our countries.[255]

Khrushchev went on to mention the Bay of Pigs, pointing out that it could be resolved by mutual cooperation:

Unfortunately, the international situation in connection with well-known events relating to Cuba has recently become somewhat heated and a definite public disagreement in the relations between our two countries has taken place.... We hope, however, that the differences which have recently arisen will be resolved in time, and that the relations between the Soviet Union and the United States will improve...[256]

Khrushchev finally accepted Kennedy's proposal for an informal meeting:

Your initiative with respect to such a meeting has found a favorable echo among us and we agree with you as to the usefulness of such an exchange of views. I confirm by this letter my acceptance of your proposal for the meeting. The time and place of the meeting as proposed are acceptable to me, namely June 3 or 4 in Vienna.[257]

Figure 33. Kennedy and Khrushchev met in Vienna on June 4, 1961. Source: JFK Presidential Library

The summit in Vienna went ahead as planned on June 4. While publicly hailed as a diplomatic triumph for the U.S., Kennedy did not feel that his attempt for a new era of cooperation was making any progress.[258] Kennedy felt that he had been bested in a fruitless ideological debate with a master debater. Commenting about the Summit and Khrushchev, he told a *New York Times* reporter that it was the "worst thing in my life. He savaged me."[259]

Kennedy's outreach to the Soviet Union would eventually bear fruit in the last months in his presidency, but not without much confrontation and crisis in the intervening period. The April, 1961, Bay of Pigs debacle had torn away the gloss of the new Kennedy administration's pledge to cooperate with the USSR in a "quest for peace."[260] In October 1962, the U.S. and USSR would come to the brink of nuclear war over the Cuban

Missile crisis. Thankfully, both sides avoided war through some adroit diplomacy. It would be less than one year later that Kennedy would again wade into the heady waters of international cooperation – this time involving cooperation in outer space.

Kennedy Proposes Joint Space and Lunar Missions with the Soviet Union

In September 1963, President Kennedy launched a ground-breaking initiative to get the USSR and USA to cooperate in joint space and lunar missions. In the background of this publicly announced initiative with powerful Cold War implications was a more secretive attempt by the Kennedy administration to gain access to classified UFO files. Leaked documents reveal that Kennedy instructed the CIA to release classified UFO files to NASA as part of the cooperative space effort with the Soviet Union. If Kennedy had succeeded, there would have been a joint space missions to the moon, and greater sharing of classified UFO files between the CIA, NASA, and the Kennedy administration. This effort would have ensured eventual public release of classified UFO files by both the U.S. and USSR.

In a stunning speech before the United Nations General Assembly on September 20, 1963, President Kennedy said:

> Finally, in a field where the United States and the Soviet Union have a special capacity -- in the field of space -- there is room for new cooperation, for further joint efforts in the regulation and exploration of space. I include among these possibilities a joint expedition to the moon.[261]

Kennedy was offering to put an end to the space race and start joint missions with the Soviets. According to Khrushchev's eldest son, Dr. Sergei Khrushchev, this was not the first time that Kennedy had proposed joint space and lunar missions with the USSR. Sergei Khrushchev revealed that at the June, 1961 Vienna Summit, less than ten days after Kennedy's famous May 25 speech before a joint session of the U.S. Congress promising to land a man on the moon before the end of the decade,[262] Kennedy secretly proposed joint space and lunar missions to his father. Khrushchev declined, as Sergei Khrushchev later explained: "My father rejected this because he thought that through this the Americans could find out how weak we were, and maybe it would push them to begin a war."[263]

Figure 34. President Kennedy addressing United Nations General Assembly. Sept 25, 1961. Source: JFK Presidential Library

In the period immediately after his September, 1963 UN speech, Khrushchev once again rebuffed Kennedy's offer – the Soviet government did not officially comment and the Soviet press ignored it.[264] At the same time, there was considerable opposition to Kennedy's initiative in both NASA and the U.S. Congress. Just before his UN speech, Kennedy briefed his NASA administrator, James Webb, about his initiative and asked: "Are you sufficiently in control to prevent my being undercut in NASA if I do that?"[265] According to official NASA history, "Webb told the president that he could keep things under control."[266] According to Richard C. Hoagland and Mike Bara:

> Selling the idea to the Soviets would be hard enough, but selling it to the American people and the Congress if there was "dissension in the ranks" might make it near impossible. If Webb couldn't hold discipline from inside NASA, the whole effort would collapse.[267]

In the weeks after bold initiative, Hoagland and Bara wrote, "the lack of public support, even within the U.S. seemed to have scuttled the idea permanently, and Kennedy began to publicly back away from his proposal."[268] If Khrushchev were to eventually accept his offer, Kennedy would need to move quickly to overcome resistance in Congress and NASA to implement any joint space agreement.

In a series of interviews beginning in 1997, Dr. Sergei Khrushchev said after his father initially refused Kennedy's September 20, 1963 offer of joint space and lunar missions, that "in the weeks after the rejection, his father had second thoughts."[269] In one interview, Sergei Khrushchev said:

> I walked with him, sometime in late October or November, and he told me about all these things. He told me that we have to think about this and maybe accept this idea. I asked why they would know everything, our secrets? He said it's not important. The Americans can design everything they want. It is a very well developed country, but we will have to save money. It's very expensive.... He thought also of the political achievement of all these things, that then they would begin to trust each other much more. After the Cuban missile crisis, his trust with President Kennedy was raised very high. He thought that it's possible to deal with this

President, he didn't think that they could be friends, but he really wanted to avoid the war, so through this co-operation they could sojourn their thoughts on these achievements.[270]

Sergei Khrushchev confirmed that his father finally accepted Kennedy's offer in early November, 1963, just over a week before his assassination.[271] According to Hoagland and Bara, the exact date can be traced to November 11 when a key Soviet Mars mission had failed: "A Mars-bound unmanned spacecraft code-named 'Cosmos 21' failed in low Earth orbit exactly one day (November 11) before Kennedy's sudden "Soviet Cooperation Directive to James Webb."[272] Khrushchev's abrupt turn-around, after two years of secret and public overtures by Kennedy, led to a series of immediate Presidential executive actions by Kennedy on the next day.

President Kennedy issued National Security Action Memorandum (NSAM) No. 271 on November 12, 1963. The subject header was "Cooperation with the USSR on Outer Space Matters," and the key passage was:

> I would like you to assume personally the initiative and central responsibility within the Government for the development of a program of substantive cooperation with the Soviet Union in the field of outer space, including the development of specific technical proposals.[273]

The Memorandum furthermore went on to say that the cooperation was a direct outcome of Kennedy's September 20 proposal "for broader cooperation between the United States and the USSR in outer space, including cooperation in lunar landing programs." The Memorandum was classified "Confidential" and addressed to James Webb (NASA Administrator). It was declassified on October 13, 1981.

UNCLASSIFIED

THE WHITE HOUSE
WASHINGTON

CONFIDENTIAL

November 12, 1963

NATIONAL SECURITY ACTION MEMORANDUM NO. 271

MEMORANDUM FOR

    The Administrator, National Aeronautics and Space
    Administration

SUBJECT: Cooperation with the USSR on Outer Space Matters

I would like you to assume personally the initiative and central
responsibility within the Government for the development of a
program of substantive cooperation with the Soviet Union in the
field of outer space, including the development of specific technical proposals. I assume that you will work closely with the
Department of State and other agencies as appropriate.

These proposals should be developed with a view to their possible discussion with the Soviet Union as a direct outcome of
my September 20 proposal for broader cooperation between
the United States and the USSR in outer space, including cooperation in lunar landing programs. All proposals or suggestions originating within the Government relating to this
general subject will be referred to you for your consideration
and evaluation.

In addition to developing substantive proposals, I expect that
you will assist the Secretary of State in exploring problems of
procedure and timing connected with holding discussions with
the Soviet Union and in proposing for my consideration the
channels which would be most desirable from our point of
view. In this connection the channel of contact developed

UNCLASSIFIED

CONFIDENTIAL

Russia oro 91 (12 Nov 63)

SecDef Control No. X1448

Figure 35. NSAM 271. Source: Majestic Documents

200

Significantly, Kennedy added: "I assume that you will work closely with the Department of State and other agencies as appropriate." Kennedy identified the Secretary of State as a key person in implementing the process by which dialogue over the cooperation would take place:

> I expect you [Webb] will assist the Secretary of State in exploring problems of procedure and timing connected with holding discussions with the Soviet Union and in proposing for my consideration the channels which would be most desirable from our point of view.[274]

This would ensure that the State Department and other U.S. government agencies would have access to the information to be shared with the Soviets under the cooperative space initiative.

In addition to the Confidential National Security Action Memorandum (NSAM), Kennedy issued a more highly classified "Top Secret" Memorandum to the Director of the CIA, John McCone. Dated the same day of November 12, 1963, the subject header of the file was: "Classification review of all UFO intelligence files affecting National Security." According to a draft of the Top Secret Memorandum that was leaked, Kennedy went on to say:

> [I] have instructed James Webb to develop a program with the Soviet Union in Joint space and lunar explorations. It would be very helpful if you would have the high threat [UFO] cases reviewed with the purpose of identification of bona fides as opposed to classified CIA and USAF sources…. When this data has been sorted out, I would like you to arrange a program of data sharing with NASA where Unknowns [UFOs] are a factor. This will

help NASA mission directors in their defensive responsibilities. I would like an interim report on the data review no later than February 1, 1964.[275]

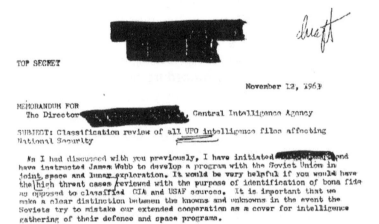

TOP SECRET

draft

November 12, 1963

MEMORANDUM FOR
The Director ▓▓▓▓▓▓▓▓▓▓, Central Intelligence Agency

SUBJECT: Classification review of all UFO intelligence files affecting National Security

As I had discussed with you previously, I have initiated ▓▓▓▓▓▓ and have instructed James Webb to develop a program with the Soviet Union in joint, space and lunar exploration. It would be very helpful if you would have the high threat cases reviewed with the purpose of identification of bona fide as opposed to classified CIA and USAF sources. It is important that we make a clear distinction between the knowns and unknowns in the event the Soviets try to mistake our extended cooperation as a cover for intelligence gathering of their defence and space programs.

When this data has been sorted out, I would like you to arrange a program of data sharing with NASA where Unknowns are a factor. This will help NASA mission directors in their defensive responsibilities.

I would like an interim report on the data review no later than February 1, 1964.

/S/ John F. Kennedy

Figure 36. Kennedy Draft Memorandum to CIA Director, McCone. Source: Majestic Documents

Kennedy's reference to classified CIA and USAF sources of UFO reports shows that he was aware that they were systematically separated into classified and unclassified files. The USAF and the other military services were secretly required to direct their most important UFO files, reported through the CIRVIS (Communications Instructions for Reporting Vital Intelligence

Sightings) system created for reporting vital intelligence data by Joint Army Air Naval Publication 146, to the CIA.[276] This is supported by a memorandum by Brigadier General C.H. Bolender on October 1969. He wrote: "reports of unidentified flying objects which could affect national security are made in accordance with JANAP 146 or Air Force Manual 55-11, and are not part of the Blue Book system."[277]

Put simply, there were two sets of UFO files being collected by the USAF during the Kennedy and later presidential administrations. Those with least national security significance were made available to the public through Project Blue Book - the "official" public investigation of UFOs by the USAF that formally ended in 1970.[278] The more important, classified UFO files, were directed into another project that was under the control of the CIA. In particular, the CIA's counterintelligence department controlled access and reported directly to the MJ-12 Group. Requesting the CIA to share UFO files with NASA, would in turn lead to its sharing this information with the State Department and other agencies as stipulated in NSAM 271. Kennedy was, therefore, directly confronting the CIA over its ultimate control of classified UFO files.

It is important to note that the Memorandum to the CIA Director refers to the National Security Action Memorandum issued to Webb on the same day. Even though the leaked Top Secret Memorandum to the CIA has not been officially acknowledged (its authenticity has been ranked medium-to-high level), [279] there is no question about the legitimacy of the National Security Action Memorandum (NSAM) 271.[280] NSAM 271 clearly showed that Kennedy had decided to cooperate with the USSR on "Outer Space Matters." If Kennedy had been warned about the dangers of future conflict with the Soviet Union and/or with extraterrestrial life, then sharing classified UFO files was an obvious way to implement NSAM 271.

NSAM 271 and the associated Top Secret Memorandum to the CIA Director issued on November 12, 1963, are evidence that Kennedy firmly linked cooperation with the USSR on "outer space matters" with the release of classified UFO files. Kennedy was aware that the CIA was the lead agency for ensuring the release of classified UFO files, not the U.S. Air Force. Project Blue Book, as many UFO researchers have rightly concluded, was a public relations exercise.[281]

Kennedy's Hotline Conversation with Nikita Khrushchev

Another leaked document shows the extent to which Kennedy was prepared to cooperate with the Soviet Union in declassifying UFO files. The aim was to avoid the risk of a mistaken military confrontation over UFOs. The document is allegedly a Top Secret NSA intercept of a "Hot Line" conversation between Kennedy and Khrushchev dated November 12, 1963.[282] The Hot Line was first established three months earlier on August 1, 1963, and according to the *New York Times*:

> The direct link, which is available 24 hours a day, will make it possible for the heads of the two Governments to exchange messages in minutes. After checking the typed message against the original copy, the Teletype tape will be fed into a Teletype transmitter. As the message goes out, it will be encoded by a "scrambling device" to prevent anyone from reading it at relay points along the 10,000-mile cable circuit. In Moscow, the message will go through a decoding device and appear on a Teletype machine in the Kremlin near the office of Premier Khrushchev.[283]

Though it is claimed the Hot Line was first used on June 5, 1967 during the six day Arab-Israeli war, the leaked NSA document suggests that Kennedy and Khrushchev used it soon after it was established.

In the alleged November 12 Hot Line conversation, Kennedy and Khrushchev discussed the importance of their respective UFO working groups dealing with the UFO issue to avoid the risk of future conflict. Kennedy told Khrushchev: "I have begun an initiative with our NASA to exchange information with your Academy of Sciences in which I hope will foster mutual concern over this problem and hopefully find some resolution."[284]

Kennedy was certainly referring to the National Security Action Memorandum (NSAM 271) released on the same day, November 12, 1963. Kennedy also said, "I have also instructed our CIA to provide me with full disclosure on the phantom aspects and classified programs in which I can better assess the [UFO] situation."[285] While the NSA intercept has not been conclusively determined to be authentic (its authenticity has been ranked medium-to-high level),[286] it is consistent with the November 12 NSAM 271."[287]

Most importantly, circumstantial evidence for the genuineness of the Hot Line transcript comes from Sergei Khrushchev's admission that his father had accepted Kennedy's offer on November 11, one day before. To repeat, this was the same day that a Soviet Mars mission 'Cosmos 21' had failed, leading to Khrushchev's change of heart about Kennedy's offer of space cooperation. For the Soviets, continuing the space race would be very expensive, and drain resources from other important areas. Kennedy's offer was a face-saving way out of the dilemma now confronting the Soviet Union.

TOP SECRET
UMBRA

NSA INTERCEPT OF THE "HOT LINE"
COMSEC FILE DATED 11/12/63

ETCRRM TX HOURLY TEST
FROM: OOTP
TO   :PUSSR
SUBJ: UFO WORKING GROUPS

WHCA
SOD
DCIA
DNSA
NMCC
CJCS
SECSTATE
NSC

"Mr. Premiere a situation has developed that affects both our
countries and the world and I feel it necessary to convey to you a
problem that we share in common."

"Mr. President I agree."

"As you must appreciate the tension between our two great nations
has often brought us to the brink of showmanship with all the
tapestry of a Greek comedy and our impasse last year was foolish
and deadly. The division that separates us is through
misunderstanding, politics, and cultural differences. But we have
one thing in common which I would like to address to your
working group on the UFO problem."

"Yes, yes...I agree with your assessment. We nearly tied the knot
that divides us permanently. Our working group believes the same
way as yours. The UFO problem presents grave dangers to our

Figure 37. NSA Hotline Intercept. P.1. Source: Majestic Documents

The Hot Line conversation shows Kennedy and Khrushchev reaching agreement on a broad range of issues concerning sharing UFOs information and joint cooperation in space. The dating of the Hot Line conversation is consistent with the agreement reached in the background over this period between Kennedy and Khrushchev. This gives more credence in the authenticity of the Hot Line document. The issuing of NSAM 271, which is an authentic official document also confirms that Khrushchev had only just accepted Kennedy's offer, and that a hotline conversation between Kennedy and Khrushchev had very likely just occurred.[288]

President Kennedy's UFO Initiatives Lead to Implementation of Assassination Directive

On November 12, 1963, President John F. Kennedy had reached broad agreement with Soviet Premier Nikita Khrushchev on joint space missions and sharing classified UFO files. This agreement required both leaders to instruct their respective UFO working groups to share information. Kennedy did this through a November 12th Top Secret memorandum to the Director of the CIA to share UFO files with NASA and the USSR. His memorandum was relayed to James Jesus Angleton who controlled access to the most highly classified UFO files in the U.S., and was in direct communications with MJ-12 - the UFO working group within the "MJ-12 Special Studies Project." In responding to Kennedy's request, Angleton followed a Top Secret/MJ-12 set of directives. One of the secret directives, revealed in the leaked and partially burned Top Secret/MJ-12 document forensically dated to 1961, was a cryptic assassination directive. In case any senior U.S. official did not cooperate with MJ-12, the directive sanctioned political assassination. The leaked document is smoking gun evidence that former CIA Director Allen Dulles was involved in drafting and approving along with six other MJ-12 members an obscure "assassination directive." The MJ-12 "assassination directive" was later implemented by Angleton in response to President Kennedy's November 12, 1963 request to the CIA to release classified UFO files.

In chapter 5, I discussed the burned document and its genesis during the final months of Allen Dulles' tenure as Director of the CIA. Dulles and other MJ-12 members were responding to Kennedy's initial effort on June 28, 1961 to be fully briefed on MJ-12 intelligence operations and UFOs. Kennedy, according to a leaked Top Secret Memorandum titled "Review of MJ-12 Intelligence Operations," requested Dulles to give a brief summary.[289] In response and unknown to Kennedy, Dulles drafted a set of directives shortly before his November ,1961 retirement.

Dulles' draft document was addressed to six members of MJ-12 requesting comments and their approval. It had clear instructions that under no circumstances would any U.S. President or his national security staff be briefed or given access to classified UFO files. While this may sound surprising to the reader, it is very common for "white world" politicians to be denied access to "black world" operations. The most common reason is to provide plausible deniability to U.S. officials in case such operations go awry. The most damning directive, drafted by Dulles and approved by six other MJ-12 members, was a cryptic assassination directive called "Project Environment."

Kennedy's 1963 efforts to end the Cold War, cooperate with the USSR on joint space missions, and share classified UFO files with the Soviets, created a final showdown with MJ-12. The trigger was Kennedy's agreement with Khrushchev on November 12, 1963 on space cooperation that led to Kennedy's Top Secret memo instructing the new Director of the CIA, John McCone, to share all UFO information with NASA.[290] Due to NSAM 271, issued the same day, this would ensure that classified UFO files would be shared not only with the USSR, but with the State Department and other U.S. agencies.[291] In short, the two memoranda Kennedy issued on November 12, would ensure that access to classified UFO files would be extended to more government agencies, ultimately resulting in direct Presidential access. Direct access had been denied to him by McCone's predecessor, Allen Dulles. Dulles had engineered a means by which he could still deny Kennedy access to UFO information, even though he was out of office.

Kennedy's explosive Top Secret November 12, 1963 memo to the CIA Director was relayed by William Colby, then (Deputy) Chief of the CIA's Far East Division, to James Angleton in CIA counterintelligence. It was Angleton who had been given the authority to implement "Project Environment" by the MJ-12 Group if the latter's operations were threatened. The trigger for implementing the Directive was a demand by the Kennedy administration for the CIA to release its classified UFO files.

On the bottom of Kennedy's Memorandum to the CIA, next to the signature space appears the following handwriting: "Response from Colby: Angleton has MJ directive 11/20/63." Colby is acknowledging that Angleton, two days before Kennedy's assassination, had the MJ directive – the burned document – and would use it to respond to Kennedy's Memorandum. This handwriting directly implicates the MJ-12 Group and Angleton in the Kennedy assassination due to the cryptic MJ-12 assassination directive.

Figure 38. Handwriting at bottom of Kennedy Memorandum to CIA Director, McCone, Nov 12, 1963. "Response from Colby – Angleton has the directive." 11/20/63. Source: Majestic Documents

CIA Counterintelligence and the Kennedy Assassination

There is more evidence to directly implicate the CIA and Angleton in the Kennedy assassination. Lee Harvey Oswald was among a small group of American citizens who defected to the Soviet Union in 1959. Though the CIA admits to having established a file on Oswald in 1960, Alan Weberman, one of the first authors to write on the Kennedy Assassination, claims that CIA counterintelligence was monitoring Oswald even earlier. Weberman cites evidence that Angleton was directly involved through an intermediary, Gerry Hemming, a former Marine who knew Oswald and was recruited by the CIA. [292]

Despite controversy over Oswald being recruited by Angleton and the CIA prior to his trip to the Soviet Union, there is no question that as an American defector, Oswald became the responsibility of Angleton's CIA counterintelligence. Upon his return to the U.S. in June 1962, Oswald's activities were closely monitored by CIA counterintelligence. Oswald's subsequent association with a number of CIA assets provided opportunities

210

for Angleton's counterintelligence to not only monitor, but to manipulate Oswald.

The most documented proof of a CIA link to the Kennedy assassination was the investigation by Jim Garrison, District Attorney of New Orleans. Garrison found much documentary evidence to demonstrate that Oswald was involved in a conspiracy led by New Orleans businessman, Clay Shaw. Garrison discovered that Shaw had an "extensive international role as an employee of the CIA."[293] While Garrison was unsuccessful in earning a conviction against Shaw, Garrison was partly vindicated in 1979 by the House Select Committee on Assassinations. The Committee concluded: "The committee believes, on the basis of the evidence available to it, that President John F. Kennedy was probably assassinated as a result of a conspiracy. The committee was unable to identify the other gunmen or the extent of the conspiracy."[294]

Smoking gun evidence for CIA involvement in the Kennedy Assassination arrived in 2007 with the explosive confession by a former CIA agent, E. Howard Hunt. Hunt confirmed that he worked as a "bench warmer" for a CIA hit team planning the assassination. His confession was taped by his son, Saint John Hunt, and first appeared in the April 5, 2007 edition of Rolling Stone Magazine.[295] Howard Hunt is best known for his role in the Watergate burglary of the Democratic National Headquarters at the Watergate Hotel. Hunt's trial and conviction captivated Washington D.C., and became known as the infamous Watergate Scandal. In one of the Nixon tapes, the disgraced former President discussed Hunt's importance insofar as he had information that could blow open what really happened in the Kennedy Assassination. Nixon told H.R. Haldeman:

> [V]ery bad, to have this fellow Hunt, ah, you know, ah, it's, he, he knows too damn much and he was involved, we happen to know that. And that it gets out that the

whole, this is all involved in the Cuban thing, that it's a fiasco, and it's going to make the FBI, ah CIA look bad, it's going to make Hunt look bad, and it's likely to blow the whole, uh, Bay of Pigs thing which we think would be very unfortunate for CIA and for the country at this time, and for American foreign policy, and he just better tough it and lay it on them. [296]

Howard Hunt confessed on tape to his son, who summarized his father's involvement in the Kennedy assassination as follows:

In 1963 my father and Frank Sturgis met with David Morales, a contract killer for the CIA, at a safe house in Miami. Morales explained that he had been picked by Bill Harvey, a rogue and unstable CIA agent with a long history of black ops, for a secret "off the board" assignment. It was Morales' understanding that this project was coming down through a chain of command starting with vice-President Lyndon Johnson. All these men shared common ground: a hatred for Kennedy. He was dangerous to their vision of America's political future, and had abandoned them in their time of need by refusing to bail out the Bay of Pigs fiasco. [297]

Support for Hunt's reference to Johnson comes from Roger Stone, a Republican strategist. He claims that Johnson micromanaged all aspects of Kennedy's route through Dallas, and ensured he would pass through Dealey Plaza. In his book, *The Man who Killed Kennedy - the case against LBJ,'* Stone concludes that Johnson set up the Kennedy assassination. [298]

The role of Vice President Johnson in the Kennedy Assassination is significant. Johnson had accompanied Kennedy on his White Sands Missile Range visit earlier in June, 1963. If Kennedy had received a classified UFO briefing, then it is significant that Johnson was there. Was Kennedy including Johnson to keep him in the loop? Or, more likely, was Johnson working with MJ-12 to monitor Kennedy's activities? In the first chapter, it was revealed that Johnson had visited the hospital suite of James Forrestal in May, 1949, against the latter's wishes. Johnson appeared to be working with a group of officials to silence Forrestal. That group, as we now know, was MJ-12. This suggests that Lyndon Johnson had, by 1963, been a Congressional asset for MJ-12 for at least 14 years.

Saint John Hunt goes on to describe how his father learned of the target for the "off the board" assignment being discussed by this band of Kennedy haters:

> "Well, I asked them what this assignment was." Sturgis looked at Morales and then at my father and calmly said: "Killing that son of a bitch Kennedy."[299]

The principal figure in recruiting the team of trained CIA assassins, according to Hunt, was a CIA agent, Cord Meyer. According to Saint John Hunt:

> Cord Myer had his own reason to hate John Kennedy. His ex-wife Mary was one of Kennedy's numerous mistresses.... After the assassination, Mary Myer was mysteriously murdered and her personal diary stolen from her apartment, allegedly by James Angleton, chief spook of counterintelligence. [300]

Once again, as in the case of Marilyn Monroe, we have a reference to Angleton spying on former mistresses of President Kennedy, and their diaries vanishing after their mysterious deaths.

According to Howard Hunt's version of events, the Kennedy assassination was codenamed the "Big Event," and was approved up an official chain of command. The "Big Event" was not a rogue operation. Kennedy's assassination by a hit team organized by CIA assets directly implicates CIA counterintelligence. Ensuring Oswald's participation in the Kennedy assassination, no matter how minimal, provided a powerful rationale for preventing a thorough investigation of the Kennedy assassination. Angleton and the CIA could persuasively argue that Oswald – a former communist defector – could directly implicate the USSR.. This allowed the CIA to successfully argue to the Warren Commission, through Allen Dulles who was a member, that a thorough investigation was too dangerous. If the Soviet Union was implicated, it risked nuclear war.

Historians who view the CIA as complicit in Kennedy's assassination point to the CIA's role in covert operations in Vietnam as the reason why the CIA wanted Kennedy's removal from office. Col. Fletcher Prouty, in his highly documented book, *JFK: The CIA, Vietnam and the Plot to Assassinate John F. Kennedy,* reveals that Kennedy was attempting to end the CIA's influence over covert operations.[301] Chief among these was the escalating U.S. involvement in Vietnam that Kennedy wanted to end. This he posits is why Kennedy was assassinated. There is, however, a more compelling reason why the CIA wanted Kennedy's removal from office - the CIA's role in controlling classified UFO information, and denying access to other government agencies including the office of the President.

The assassination of President Kennedy was the direct result of his efforts to gain access to the CIA's control of classified UFO files. Unknown to Kennedy, a set of secret MJ-12 directives issued by his former CIA Director, Allen Dulles, ruled out any cooperation with Kennedy and his National Security staff on the UFO issue. It was Dulles and another six MJ-12 Group members who sanctioned the directives found in the burned document, including a vague political assassination directive against non-cooperative officials in the Kennedy administration. This could be applied to Kennedy himself if the official entrusted to carry out the MJ-12 Assassination Directive concluded the President threatened MJ-12 operations.

In chapter 6, I analyzed the initial composition of the MJ-12 Group described in the Eisenhower Briefing Document, and put together a list of the most likely members of MJ-12 Group during the Kennedy administration. Furthermore, I showed who among the twelve were most likely to have been part of a sub-group of six that approved by consensus, the set of directives drafted by Allen Dulles who was MJ-1 at the time. Among the directives was an "Assassination Directive." It is very likely that this was the directive that Angleton had in his possession and was going to implement according to William Colby's handwritten comment on Kennedy's November 12, 1963 Top Secret Memorandum to John McCone. Consequently, here is the list of individuals that may have been among the total of seven MJ-12 Group members that approved the Assassination Directive in 1961 to be used against any U.S. political figure that threatened MJ-12 operations: Allen Dulles (MJ-1); Dr Edward Teller (MJ-2); Lt General Marshall Carter (MJ-3); General Curtis LeMay (MJ-4); General Gordon Blake (MJ-5); Dr Detlev Bronk (MJ-6); and Dr Jerome Hunsaker (MJ-7).

While Dulles and his six associates pre-authorized the assassination of any political figure who threatened MJ-12 Group operations in late 1961, it would be implemented much later in the Kennedy Administration. The Assassination Directive had been passed on to Dulles' close ally James Jesus Angleton, the CIA counterintelligence chief, for safekeeping and possible implementation. Even though he would no longer be CIA Director, Dulles had engineered a means whereby he would still be able to deny Kennedy access to the CIA's classified UFO files – even deprive Kennedy of his life, if he demanded access to them.

It was Kennedy's joint space cooperation initiative with the USSR and the demand that the CIA share all UFO information with NASA, the State Department and the Soviets that was the trigger that put the assassination plan into action. Kennedy's November 12, 1963 Memorandum to CIA Director McCone for the CIA to share UFO information, was judged to be a direct threat to MJ-12 Group operations. Colby's handwritten reference to Angleton having the directive is very significant. It reveals that Angleton, in his official capacity as head of the CIA's counterintelligence division and safe-keeper of the classified UFO files, was authorized to respond to any UFO ultimatum by the Kennedy administration.

Angleton consequently made the decision to go ahead with the implementation of the Assassination Directive according to the classified instructions he received when the Directive has been entrusted to him by Dulles in late 1961. The Directive had by then been approved by the MJ-Group to whom Angleton ultimately answered. The Assassination Directive had been written cryptically, thereby insulating the MJ-12 Group from possible blowback in the case of a leak. A seasoned covert operative like Angleton knew its real meaning. It was Angleton who gave the orders for assembling a CIA hit team that would assassinate President Kennedy in accord with a set of cryptic instructions he had received in late 1961 by the MJ-12 Group.

Endnotes Chapter 9

[250] John F Kennedy Inaugural Address, January 20, 1961. Source: http://www.jfklibrary.org/Asset-Viewer/BqXIEM9F4024ntFl7SVAjA.aspx
[251] John F Kennedy Inaugural Address, January 20, 1961. Source: http://www.jfklibrary.org/Asset-Viewer/BqXIEM9F4024ntFl7SVAjA.aspx
[252] John F Kennedy Inaugural Address, January 20, 1961. Source: http://www.jfklibrary.org/Asset-Viewer/BqXIEM9F4024ntFl7SVAjA.aspx
[253] Source: Kennedy Presidential Library, http://www.jfklibrary.org/Asset-Viewer/Archives/JFKPOF-126-014.aspx
[254] NSAM 55-57 placed Cold War operations firmly under the control of the Joint Chiefs Available online at: http://www.jfklibrary.org/Historical+Resources/Archives/Reference+Desk/NSAMs.htm
[255] Source: Kennedy Presidential Library, http://www.jfklibrary.org/Asset-Viewer/Archives/JFKPOF-126-014.aspx
[256] Source: Kennedy Presidential Library, http://www.jfklibrary.org/Asset-Viewer/Archives/JFKPOF-126-014.aspx
[257] Source: Kennedy Presidential Library, http://www.jfklibrary.org/Asset-Viewer/Archives/JFKPOF-126-014.aspx
[258] Source: http://en.wikipedia.org/wiki/Vienna_summit#Outcomes
[259] Frederick Kempe. *Berlin 1961*. (Penguin Group 2011) 257.
[260] John F Kennedy Inaugural Address, January 20, 1961. Source: http://www.jfklibrary.org/Asset-Viewer/BqXIEM9F4024ntFl7SVAjA.aspx
[261] Address Before the 18th General Assembly of the United Nations (September 20, 1963). Available at: http://www.jfklibrary.org/Historical+Resources/Archives/Reference+Desk/Speeches/JFK/003POF03_18thGeneralAssembly09201963.htm
[262] See: http://history.nasa.gov/moondec.html
[263] Source: http://www.pbs.org/redfiles/moon/deep/interv/m_int_sergei_khrushchev.htm
[264] "The Kennedy Proposal for a Joint Moon Flight," http://history.nasa.gov/SP-4209/ch2-4.htm
[265] "The Kennedy Proposal for a Joint Moon Flight," http://history.nasa.gov/SP-4209/ch2-4.htm
[266] "The Kennedy Proposal for a Joint Moon Flight," http://history.nasa.gov/SP-4209/ch2-4.htm
[267] Richard C. Hoagland and Mike Bara, *Dark Mission: The Secret History of NASA* (Feral House, 2007) 98.
[268] Hoagland and Bara, *Dark Mission*, 89.
[269] Available online at: http://www.spacewar.com/news/russia-97h.html

[270] Available online at:
http://www.pbs.org/redfiles/moon/deep/moon_deep_inter_frm.htm
[271] Frank Sietzen, "Soviets Planned to Accept JFK's Joint Lunar Mission Offer,"
http://www.spacewar.com/news/russia-97h.html
[272] Hoagland and Bara, *Dark Mission,* 101.
[273] Available online at: http://tinyurl.com/mejpm4
[274] Available online at: http://tinyurl.com/mejpm4
[275] Available online at:
http://www.majesticdocuments.com/pdf/kennedy_cia.pdf
[276] See: http://www.cufon.org/cufon/janp1462.htm
[277] "The Bolender Memo, Oct 20, 1969,"
http://www.nicap.org/Bolender_Memo.htm
[278] For information on Project Blue Book, go to:
http://www.ufocasebook.com/bluebook.html
[279] For rating system used by the founders of the Majestic Documents website, go to: http://majesticdocuments.com/documents/authenticity.php
[280] Available online at: http://tinyurl.com/mejpm4
[281] Leading UFO researcher Allen Hynek claimed that after the departure of Captain Ruppelt, Hynek "Project Blue Book was little more than a public relations exercise." http://en.wikipedia.org/wiki/J._Allen_Hynek
[282] Available online at: http://www.majesticdocuments.com/pdf/umbra.pdf
[283] Cited at: http://deadpresidentsdaily.blogspot.com/2007/08/august-30-1963-hot-line-established.html
[284] Available online at: http://www.majesticdocuments.com/pdf/umbra.pdf
[285] Available online at: http://www.majesticdocuments.com/pdf/umbra.pdf
[286] For rating system used by the founders of the Majestic Documents website, go to: http://majesticdocuments.com/documents/authenticity.php
[287] Available online at: http://tinyurl.com/mejpm4
[288] Available online at: http://tinyurl.com/mejpm4
[289] Available online at:
http://www.majesticdocuments.com/pdf/kennedy_ciadirector.pdf
[290] Available online at:
http://www.majesticdocuments.com/pdf/kennedy_cia.pdf
[291] NSAM 271 available online at: http://tinyurl.com/mejpm4
[292] Cited online at: http://ajweberman.com/nodules2/nodulec5.htm
[293] Cited online at: http://en.wikipedia.org/wiki/Clay_Shaw
[294] Report of the Select Committee on Assassinations of the U.S. House of Representatives, available online at:
http://www.archives.gov/research/jfk/select-committee-report/summary.html
[295] It was also included in Saint John Hunt, *Bond of Secrecy: My Life with CIA Spy and Watergate Conspirator E. Howard Hunt* (Trine Day, 2012)

[296] Transcript of a Recording of a Meeting Between the President and H. R. Haldeman, the Oval Office, June 23, 1972.

[297] Hunt, *Bond of Secrecy*. Kindle Edition

[298] See Roger Stone *The Man who killed Kennedy - the case against LBJ,'* (Skyhorse Publishing, 2013). For review, go to: http://tinyurl.com/c3rae6n

[299] Hunt, *Bond of Secrecy*. Kindle Edition

[300] Hunt, *Bond of Secrecy*. Kindle Edition

[301] Fletcher Prouty, *JFK: The CIA, Vietnam and the Plot to Assassinate John F. Kennedy* (Citadel; 2003 [1996]).

Chapter 10

Kennedy's Last Stand

President Clinton wanted answers to two questions: "One, who killed JFK. And two, are there UFOs?"[302] Webster Hubbell, his close friend and Associate Justice at the Department of Justice, couldn't find satisfactory answers. Based on the evidence and documents examined in this book, this is what I would tell Clinton.

President Kennedy's decision to demand the sharing of the CIA's classified UFO files on November 12, 1963 was his last stand against the Majestic-12 Group. Majestic-12, through its surrogates in the CIA, had systematically denied the Kennedy administration access to its classified UFO files and projects at its prized S-4 facility at Area 51. Kennedy had made many attempts to gain access soon after beginning his term of office. Confronting a similar problem only five years earlier, President Eisenhower decided he would threaten to use the U.S. First Army against the MJ-12 Group. MJ-12 understood well the credible military threat posed by Eisenhower and relented. Eisenhower had succeeded in his battle to get the information he requested.

By the end of his administration, Eisenhower understood that he had lost the war against the expanding power of MJ-12. In his farewell speech, he could only vaguely warn about the dangers posed to American "liberties and democratic processes" posed by the military-industrial complex.[303] In reality, he had something much more specific in mind about the threat to America. In private meetings with President-Kennedy, Eisenhower shared the truth. The Majestic-12 Group was a growing menace and had to be stopped.

Kennedy had prior knowledge of the UFO issue from his time as an intelligence officer with the Office of Naval Intelligence during the Los Angeles Air Raid incident in February, 1942. This information was augmented by his friendship and working relationship with former Secretary of Defense, James Forrestal. Kennedy traveled to post-War Germany in July and August, 1945 as a guest of Forrestal who at the time was Secretary of the Navy. Forrestal gave Kennedy access to military and political leaders at the highest level. In his diaries, *Prelude to Leadership*, Kennedy wrote about his meetings and examination of various Nazi technologies. He helped Forrestal determine which of these might benefit the U.S. Navy.

During Kennedy's visit to the Potsdam Conference with Forrestal in late July, 1945, he observed policy decisions being made by President Truman, Prime Minister Churchill and Premier Stalin. He also observed the discussions General Eisenhower and U.S. military government authorities had with Truman. President Truman made the formal decision in August to approve the repatriation of former Nazi scientists and technologies under Operation Paperclip, soon after his visit to Germany and the Potsdam conference. Some of these technologies involved flying saucer designs that were allegedly extraterrestrial in origin.

Operation Paperclip was run by the Joint Intelligence Objectives Agency that comprised military intelligence officers from each of the military services.[304] In his official capacity as Secretary of the Navy, Forrestal was aware of Operation Paperclip and its significance. He gave Kennedy full access to this level of information during their 1945 German tour. Forrestal hoped to recruit Kennedy to his personal staff, but ultimately Kennedy decided to enter politics. Forrestal rose to become the first Secretary of Defense, and a founding member of the Majestic-12 Group.

In 1947, Kennedy learned about the Roswell crash while serving in his freshman year as a Congressman. He received an informal briefing that had been approved by either the Secretary of the Air Force, Stuart Symington, and/or from Secretary Forrestal. With his Naval Intelligence background, Kennedy understood how psychological warfare operated. The 1947 Roswell UFO Crash was the start of a massive psychological warfare operation against the American and World public. While a Congressman, Kennedy's briefing of the Roswell crash may have been approved to recruit his support for the cover-up of UFOs and extraterrestrial life.

Forrestal's importance in passing on information about UFOs and extraterrestrial life to Kennedy cannot be overstated. As a founding member of the Majestic-12 Group, Forrestal had full access to information, and participated in major policy decisions. Apparently, the cover-up policy was something Forrestal strongly disagreed with, and he began briefing members of Congress about what was really happening. Kennedy almost certainly would have been among those with whom Forrestal was sharing this information. Forrestal's actions had become a cause of concern for Truman and he decided to remove Forrestal from office in March, 1949. Only two months later, Forrestal was dead. The official story that Forrestal had suffered a mental breakdown was a lie. He was giving unauthorized briefings about UFOs and extraterrestrial life. Truman and MJ-12 decided that Forrestal had to be silenced.

Forrestal's death in May, 1949, was the first instance of a senior political figure being killed to maintain the UFO cover-up. Forrestal's death weighed heavily on Kennedy. Forrestal had introduced Kennedy to the highest levels of governmental policy-making in 1945. Kennedy had been given access to many official secrets by Forrestal, including the full significance of Operation Paperclip. Even though Kennedy chose to enter politics, they remained firm friends and ideological allies.

Forrestal's son, Michael, served in the Kennedy administration as a leading aid to National Security Advisor, McGeorge Bundy.

The knowledge Kennedy acquired from James Forrestal, and while serving in Congress, would help him greatly as he developed a number of initiatives to learn about MJ-12 Group operations dealing with UFOs and extraterrestrial life. He understood that Cold War psychological operations were a cover for Majestic-12 Group operations. Kennedy immediately set about placing all Cold War psychological operations under the control of his national security team with the issue of his Executive Order in February 1961, abolishing the Operations Coordinating Board.

Kennedy's resolve to assert Presidential authority over psychological warfare operations and to get to the bottom of the UFO issue would not go unchallenged. His effort to get CIA Director Dulles to share information about the MJ-12 Group and its psychological warfare operations was unsuccessful. Unlike Eisenhower before him, Kennedy could not use the threat of commanding the U.S. Army to invade Area 51. Top Pentagon leaders were not favorably disposed to the Kennedy administration, especially after the Bay of Pigs fiasco in April 1961. Kennedy had to come up with another strategy, which was an end-run around the CIA.

Using his power as Commander-in-Chief, Kennedy visited various military facilities to see what they possessed in terms of alien artifacts. He was receiving secret UFO briefings, relayed through his brother Bobby, from the head of the U.S. Army's Research and Development Division, Lt. Colonel Corso, about reverse engineering alien technologies. Kennedy possibly met with one of the leading UFO contactees of the era; and received communications from and perhaps met with human-looking extraterrestrials. If rumors were true that James Forrestal had also been a contactee, then he would have undoubtedly shared this information with Kennedy.

Kennedy shared some of the UFO information he had learned with Marilyn Monroe during various trysts with her. When he and Bobby were warned by FBI Director Hoover to end their associations with Monroe, because she posed a national security threat, they did so. This, however, infuriated Monroe who had already shared some of the information Kennedy had told her with other people. She planned to go ahead with a tell-all Press conference. Unknown to Monroe, she was being monitored by the CIA's counterintelligence chief, James Angleton. He had the resources to stop her, if the Kennedys couldn't.

In a final attempt to persuade Monroe not to share the Kennedy brothers' secrets, Bobby visited her on the last day of her life. Shortly after his second visit on that fateful day, Monroe died. Unknown to Bobby Kennedy, one of the two agents accompanying him had been recruited by Angleton's counterintelligence team. He administered a lethal dose of barbiturates to Monroe, thereby directly implicating Kennedy in her death. This allowed Angleton's patrons to blackmail Bobby Kennedy, and ensure his future silence in case Angleton had to take action against his brother.

On May 28, 1963, President Kennedy visited the grave of his former mentor, James Forrestal. The visit was highly significant. Forrestal's death had been caused by his attempt to undermine the UFO cover-up. Kennedy was aware of this and was making a momentous choice to move more aggressively confronting the MJ-12 Group. Kennedy was certain that he would succeed where Forrestal had failed. Perhaps the visit was to silently express his solidarity with Forrestal's vision, and to express his resolve to help realize it.

Whether out of first-hand experience as a contactee, or from intellectual conviction based on his access to classified information, Forrestal envisioned a world where humanity knew the truth. Humanity was not alone - we were being visited by advanced civilizations from other worlds. During the three and half years of his friendship with Kennedy (1945-1949), Forrestal shared his vision. He sought to realize it and fought against those who wanted to maintain secrecy. For this Forrestal paid the ultimate price. Forrestal's vision resonated with Kennedy's own intellectual belief about the importance of government transparency and opposition to secrecy. Forrestal had first worked as a journalist. He took seriously the need for a free and open press corps. This was the safest way of monitoring government practices and preventing excesses. Forrestal's influence is apparent in Kennedy's famous April, 1961 speech advocating freedom of the press:

> The very word "secrecy" is repugnant in a free and open society; and we are as a people inherently and historically opposed to secret societies, to secret oaths and secret proceedings. We decided long ago that the dangers of excessive and unwarranted concealment of pertinent facts far outweighed the dangers which are cited to justify it. Even today, there is little value in opposing the threat of a closed society by imitating its arbitrary restrictions. Even today, there is little value in insuring the survival of our nation if our traditions do not survive with it. And there is very grave danger that an announced need for increased security will be seized upon those anxious to expand its meaning to the very limits of official censorship and concealment. That I do not intend to permit to the extent that it is in my control. And no official of my Administration, whether his rank is high or low, civilian or military, should interpret my words here tonight as an excuse to censor the news, to stifle dissent, to cover up our mistakes or to withhold from the press and the public the facts they deserve to know.[305]

One week after visiting Forrestal's grave, Kennedy would travel to the contiguous military facilities at White Sands Missile Base, Holloman Air Force Base and Fort Bliss. White Sands was where former Nazi scientists were working – most of whom had arrived under Operation Paperclip. This was one of the locations where extraterrestrial artifacts had been taken from the Roswell crash. Kennedy hoped that he would learn more about current alien-related projects and technologies. He was given a classified UFO briefing, and was accompanied by Vice President Johnson.

Among President Kennedy's final executive actions was a decision to cooperate with the Soviet Union in joint space and lunar missions. The decision by Soviet Premier Khrushchev to accept Kennedy's offer on November 11, 1963, led to Kennedy authorizing a memorandum one day later to NASA administrator, James Webb, to begin sharing information. Kennedy's National Security Action Memorandum 271, is publicly known. Less known is a leaked document allegedly of Kennedy's Top Secret Memorandum to CIA Director McCone, about sharing classified CIA files on UFOs with a number of U.S. government agencies and the Soviet Union. The extensive data sharing required under National Security Action Memorandum 271 would have given Kennedy and his National Security team a means of gaining access to classified UFO files. Kennedy's actions threatened to subvert the power and authority of the "black world" of covert operations and psychological warfare on the issue of extraterrestrial life.

Kennedy's Memorandum to McCone was a trigger for the implementation of a Draft set of Directives adopted in late 1961 by the Majestic-12 Group while Allen Dulles was still CIA Director. Acting in his capacity as the head of MJ-12, Dulles engineered a means whereby Kennedy could be denied access to the CIA's classified UFO files and projects at S-4 well after Dulles' departure as DCI. Dulles, together with six other members of the MJ-12 Group, consensually adopted a draft set of directives, including a cryptic assassination directive called "Project Environment," that could be used against any U.S. official that threatened MJ-12 Group operations.

In late 1961, MJ-12 members that approved Project Environment were most likely: Allen Dulles (MJ-1); Dr. Edward Teller (MJ-2); Lt General Marshal Carter (MJ-3); General Curtis LeMay (MJ-4); Lt General Gordon Blake (MJ-5); Dr. Detlev Bronk (MJ-6); and Dr. Jerome Hunsaker (MJ-7). The passage of "Project Environment" meant no American President would ever be able to use a threat similar to Eisenhower's of invading Area 51 to learn about MJ-12 Group operations involving extraterrestrial life and technologies. Vice-President Lyndon Johnson had been a congressional asset of MJ-12 since at least 1949. In the event that "Project Environment" was implemented, his cooperation was already assured. Johnson's cooperation was critical, especially if, as Hunt's confession suggests, action was to be taken during Kennedy's upcoming visit to Dallas.

While Kennedy didn't threaten to invade Area 51 with the U.S. Army, his directive to John McCone to share CIA files on UFOs with other U.S. agencies and the USSR was seen as a direct threat to MJ-12 Group operations. The directives had been entrusted to the head of the CIA's counterintelligence division for possible implementation if the situation required.

James Jesus Angleton acted as the official gatekeeper for the CIA's UFO secrets. He had an extensive international network for learning about UFO extraterrestrial activity anywhere on the planet. Anyone with knowledge about extraterrestrial life and technology would be monitored by Angleton's CI division. The MJ-12 Group's assassination directive gave Angleton a license to kill. If anyone threatened to reveal classified UFO secrets, they would be eliminated using any of the CIA's well trained assassins. This had earlier been the fates of

James Forrestal and Marilyn Monroe; it now became the fate of President John F. Kennedy.

Endnote Chapter 10

[302] Webster Hubbell, *Friends in High Places: Our Journey from Little Rock to Washington, D.C.* (William Morrow and Co., 1997).
[303] Eisenhower's Farewell Speech", available online at: http://mcadams.posc.mu.edu/ike.htm
[304] See http://www.archives.gov/iwg/declassified-records/rg-330-defense-secretary/
[305] Transcript available online at: http://www.thepowerhour.com/news3/jfk_speech_transcript.htm

Index

Alamogordo Army Air
    Field, 40
Angleton, James Jesus, 74,
    81, 90, 115, 116, 117,
    121, 129, 143, 179, 180,
    183, 184, 207, 208, 209,
    210, 211, 213, 214, 215,
    216, 225, 228
Area 51, 7, 70, 72, 73, 74,
    76, 78, 79, 81, 82, 83, 84,
    85, 86, 87, 91, 94, 107,
    120, 122, 135, 221, 224,
    228
Arkansas, 2, 5
Army Chief of Staff, 6, 34,
    40, 47, 50, 68, 102, 103
Army counter intelligence,
    45
assassination directive, 8,
    120, 121, 207, 208, 209,
    214
atomic bomb, 131
Attorney General, 1, 146,
    149, 159, 164, 165, 169,
    177, 184
Bay of Pigs, 2, 112, 119,
    192, 193, 194, 195, 212,
    224
Berlitz, Charles, 35, 57, 62,
    88
Blake, Gordon, 135, 141,
    143, 215

Blanchard, William, 36, 37,
    38, 39
Bluebook, Project, 99
Brazel, Mack, 34, 36, 52
Bronk, Detlev, 135, 136,
    141, 215
Burisch, Dan, 78, 79, 89, 90,
    132
Burleson, Don, 163, 166,
    170, 180, 181, 182, 186,
    187
burned document. *See*
    burned memo
Bush, Vannevar, 23, 32, 60,
    62, 66, 68, 88, 131, 141,
    143
Bush, Vannvar, 60
California, 154
Cameron, Grant, 5, 10, 99,
    146, 157
Carey, Thomas, 36, 57
Carter, Marshall, 133, 141,
    215
Catchers of Heaven
    Michael Wolf, 80, 90
Chase Brandon, 4
Cheney, Dick, 77, 89
CIA, 2, 4, 7, 8, 9, 65, 70, 72,
    73, 74, 75, 77, 78, 81, 82,
    83, 84, 85, 86, 87, 89, 91,
    107, 110, 111, 112, 115,
    116, 117, 119, 120, 121,
    122, 124, 125, 129, 130,

132, 133, 145, 146, 148, 149, 150, 155, 156, 159, 175, 178, 179, 180, 181, 182, 184, 191, 192, 196, 201, 202, 203, 205, 207, 208, 209, 210, 211, 212, 213, 214, 215, 216, 218, 219, 221, 224, 225, 227, 228

Clinton, Bill, 1, 2, 3, 4, 5, 10, 221

Clinton, Hillary, 3, 10

Colby, William, 129, 143, 209, 215, 216

Congress, U.S., 44, 45, 82, 83, 84, 91, 98, 99, 103, 145, 193, 197, 198, 224

Connecticut, 81

Cooper, Timothy, 117, 125, 155

Cornine, Lance, 48, 49

Corso, Philip, 147, 148, 155, 157, 224

Counter-Intelligence Corps, 45, 57, 58

Cuba, 168, 177, 191, 192, 194

Cutler, Robert, 65, 66, 68

Dilettoso, Mim, 80

Directorate of Intelligence, 49, 50

Dulles, Allen, 7, 74, 110, 112, 113, 115, 117, 119, 120, 121, 122, 123, 127, 128, 129, 130, 132, 134, 136, 137, 138, 140, 141,

145, 191, 192, 207, 208, 209, 214, 215, 216, 224, 227

Eisenhower Briefing Document, 60, 61, 62, 65, 66, 68, 71, 88, 109, 127, 130, 131, 136, 143, 215

Eisenhower, Dwight, 6, 7, 9, 33, 34, 40, 41, 42, 47, 48, 53, 55, 56, 59, 60, 61, 62, 65, 66, 68, 69, 70, 71, 72, 83, 84, 85, 86, 87, 88, 91, 93, 94, 95, 96, 97, 98, 99, 100, 101, 102, 103, 104, 105, 106, 107, 109, 120, 121, 122, 127, 128, 130, 131, 133, 135, 136, 137, 138, 139, 140, 141, 143, 145, 147, 189, 192, 193, 215, 221, 224, 228, 230

Element 115, 76, 89

Exopolitics, iv

Exopolitics Institute, iv

Flying Saucer Crash, 33, 34, 40

Forrestal, James, xv, 6, 11, 12, 13, 14, 15, 21, 22, 23, 24, 25, 26, 27, 28, 29, 30, 44, 54, 60, 62, 95, 132, 141, 222, 223, 224, 225

Fouche, Edgar, 81, 90

Friedman, Stanton, 35, 60, 61, 62, 65, 66, 88, 131, 135, 136, 138, 143

Frost, Laurence, 137, 141

Germany, 40

Gibbons, Jack, 3
Good, Timothy, 49, 58, 149,
150, 153, 157
Gray extraterrestrials, 78
Gray, Gordon, 137, 141
Greer, Stephen, 99, 106,
179, 183, 186, 187
Groom Lake
Area 51, 72, 74, 77, 82, 83
Haut, Walter, 35, 36, 37, 38,
39, 51, 52, 53, 54, 57, 58
Hawaii, iii
Hennessy, Derek, 76, 77
Hillenkoetter, Roscoe, 65,
130, 141
Holloman AFB, 40
Hong Kong, 3, 10
Howe, Linda Moulton, 2, 6,
10, 31, 32
Hubbell, Webster, 1, 2, 3, 4,
5, 10, 230
Hunsaker, Jerome, 65, 136,
141, 215
Interplanetary Phenomenon
Unit, 43, 45, 47, 48, 50,
51, 52, 53, 55, 102, 139
Irish Americans, 43
Jefferies, Norman, 168, 171,
172, 173, 174, 184
Johnson, Louis, 47, 72, 132
Johnson, Lyndon Baines, 24,
25, 47, 151, 212
Joint Chiefs of Staff, 7, 67,
68, 109, 110, 112, 113,
122, 134, 193
J-Rod, 78

Kennedy assassination, 2, 5,
123, 209, 210, 211, 214
Kennedy, Bobby, 8, 147,
148, 161, 164, 165, 166,
167, 168, 169, 170, 171,
172, 173, 174, 224, 225
Kennedy, Bobby., 169, 170
Kennedy, John F., 1, 2, 5, 6,
7, 8, 9, 10, 11, 33, 34, 42,
43, 44, 45, 46, 47, 51, 53,
54, 55, 93, 94, 95, 96, 98,
101, 102, 103, 104, 105,
106, 107, 108, 109, 110,
111, 112, 113, 115, 117,
118, 119, 120, 121, 122,
123, 125, 127, 129, 132,
134, 138, 141, 145, 146,
147, 148, 149, 150, 152,
153, 154, 155, 156, 157,
159, 160, 161, 162, 163,
164, 165, 166, 167, 168,
169, 170, 171, 172, 173,
174, 175, 177, 178, 180,
183, 184, 185, 189, 190,
191, 192, 193, 194, 195,
196, 197, 198, 199, 201,
202, 203, 204, 205, 207,
208, 209, 210, 211, 212,
213, 214, 215, 216, 217,
219, 221, 222, 223, 224,
225, 227, 228, 229
Kennedy, Joseph, 45
KGB, 121
Kilgannen, Dorothy, 178
Kolta, 80
Lazar, Robert, 76, 89, 132

LeMay, Curtis, 134, 141, 215
Los Angeles, 50, 168, 169, 184
Lovekin, Stephen, 98, 99, 100, 101, 103, 106
Majestic, 7, 9, 57, 60, 62, 65, 66, 67, 68, 70, 73, 74, 80, 88, 94, 104, 107, 109, 110, 113, 116, 124, 127, 128, 130, 131, 136, 143, 145, 179, 187, 218, 221, 224, 227
Marcel, Jesse, 35, 36, 37, 38, 52, 57, 62
Massachusetts, 43, 45, 47, 55
McCone, John, 129, 201, 208, 209, 215, 216, 227, 228
McConnell, Mike, 79
Menzel, Donald, 138, 141
Messuziere
Philippe de la, 81, 90
MJ-1, 78, 127, 128, 130, 141, 215
MJ-12 Special Studies Project, 7, 9, 66, 119, 207
MJ-12 SSP, 66
Monroe, Marilyn, 8, 149, 150, 156, 159, 160, 161, 162, 163, 164, 165, 166, 167, 168, 169, 170, 171, 172, 174, 175, 177, 178, 179, 180, 181, 182, 183,

184, 185, 186, 187, 213, 225, 229
Montague, Robert, 138, 139, 141
Moon Dust, Project, 182, 183
Moore, William, 35, 57, 62, 88, 162
Murray, Eunice, 168, 170, 171, 172, 173, 174, 184
National Security Action Memorandum, 119, 122, 199, 201, 203, 205, 227
National Security Agency, 133, 135, 137, 139, 179
Naval intelligence, US, 2, 18, 22
Nazi, 15, 31, 71, 73
Odom, William, 179
Operation Paperclip, 31, 40, 57
Oppenheimer, Robert, 131
Pentagon, 8, 36, 39, 68, 71, 75, 109, 122, 153, 154, 193, 224
Perret, Geoffry, 98
Puthoff, Hal, 81, 90
Ramey, Roger, 36, 37, 39, 134
Red Diary, 166, 169, 183
Republican Party, 59
Rockefeller, Laurence, 3, 141
Roosevelt, Franklin, 50, 59
Roswell, 4, 5, 6, 9, 33, 34, 35, 36, 37, 38, 39, 40, 41,

42, 43, 45, 47, 48, 50, 51,
52, 53, 54, 56, 57, 68, 71,
88, 95, 102, 103, 116,
133, 134, 135, 139, 145,
147, 149, 157, 178, 223
Roswell Army Air Field, 33,
34
Rothberg, Howard, 175,
177
S-4, 7, 59, 75, 76, 77, 78, 79,
80, 81, 82, 83, 84, 85, 86,
87, 89, 94, 101, 104, 107,
120, 122, 132, 135, 145,
221, 227
Salla, Dr Michael, iv
Samford, John, 139, 141
Schmitt, Donald, 36, 57
Secretary for Air Force, 45,
47
Shulgen, General, 180, 181
Smith, Walter, 23, 32, 59,
66, 68, 88, 106, 128, 130,
132, 133, 141
Souers, Sidney, 137, 141
Steinman, William, 48
Stevens, Wendelle, 76
Stone, Clifford, 182, 187
Summers, Anthony, 161,
162, 170, 171, 172
Symington, 47, 57, 58

Teller, Edward, 131, 132,
141, 215
Trudeau, Arthur, 147, 148
Truman, Harry, 7, 23, 40,
42, 48, 54, 55, 60, 61, 62,
66, 68, 87, 88, 108, 109,
124, 128, 131, 132, 137,
141
Twining, Nathan, 40, 41, 42,
47, 48, 55, 65, 66, 68,
133, 134, 141, 181
Unumpentium, 76
US Air Force, 47, 73, 134,
153, 181, 182, 204
Vandenberg, Hoyt, 134, 135,
141
White House Army
Signaling Agency, 98
White Sands Missile Base,
42
Wilson, Steve, 77, 78, 89
Wolf, Michael Kruvant, 80
Wolfe, Donald, 163, 167,
168, 172
Wood, Robert and Ryan, 50,
57, 58, 109, 117, 121, 124
World War II, 2, 53, 65, 131
Wright-Patterson AFB, 40,
71, 73, 85, 116, 133, 134,
135

About the Author

Dr. Michael Salla is an internationally recognized scholar in international politics, conflict resolution and U.S. foreign policy. He has held academic appointments in the School of International Service & the Center for Global Peace, American University, Washington DC (1996-2004); the Department of Political Science, Australian National  University, Canberra, Australia (1994-96); and the Elliott School of International Affairs, George Washington University, Washington D.C., (2002). He has a Ph.D in Government from the University of Queensland, Australia. During his academic career he was author/editor of four books focusing on international politics (*see next page for his book titles*). He has conducted research and fieldwork in ethnic conflicts involving East Timor, Kosovo, Macedonia, and Sri Lanka. He has been awarded significant financial grants from the United States Institute of Peace and the Ford Foundation for peacemaking initiatives involving mid-to-high level participants from the East Timor conflict.

Dr. Salla is more popularly known as a pioneer in the development of 'exopolitics', the study of the main actors, institutions and political processes associated with extraterrestrial life. He wrote the first published book on 'exopolitics' in 2004. He authored two additional exopolitics books in 2009 and early 2013. He is Founder of the *Exopolitics Institute*, and the *Exopolitics Journal*, and Co-Organizer of the *Earth Transformation* series of conferences in Hawaii (2006-2011). He is also the news anchor of ExoNews.TV a popular Youtube channel. His main website is: www.exopolitics.org

Other Books by Michael E. Salla, Ph.D

Galactic Diplomacy: Getting to Yes with ET (Exopolitics Institute, 2013)

Exposing U.S. Government Policies on Extraterrestrial Life: The Challenge of Exopolitics (Exopolitics Institute, 2009)

Exopolitics: Political Implications of the Extraterrestrial Presence (Dandelion Books, 2004)

The Hero's Journey Toward a Second American Century (Greenwood Press, 2002)

Co-Editor, *Essays on Peace* (Central Queensland University Press, 1995)

Co-Editor, *Why the Cold War Ended* (Greenwood Press, 1995)

Islamic Radicalism, Muslim Nations and the West (Indian Ocean Center for Peace Studies, 1993)

CPSIA information can be obtained
at www.ICGtesting.com
Printed in the USA
BVHW091732031118
531458BV00002BA/6/P